JANE LIDDIARD and MOLLIE HEMENS

Stepping Up
Four Play Scripts for the Classroom

Activities linked to the National Curriculum by Jane Liddiard and Mollie Hemens

Heinemann Educational Publishers
Halley Court, Jordan Hill, Oxford OX2 8EJ
Part of Harcourt Education

Heinemann is the registered trademark of Harcourt Educational Limited

First published 1996

06 05 04 03
12 11 10 9 8

ISBN 0 435 23322 X

Original design by Jeffrey White Creative Associates
Typeset by Books Unlimited (Nottm)
Cover illustration by Joan Carlass
Cover design by Aricot Vert
Printed in the UK by Clays Ltd, St Ives plc

CAUTION

**All rights whatsoever in these plays are strictly reserved
and on no account may performances be given unless written
permission has been obtained before rehearsals commence
from Heinemann Educational Publishers.**

CONTENTS

ACKNOWLEDGEMENTS

Our thanks for their help, support, and encouragement to: Anthony Hemens, John Liddiard, Ann Lovelace, Fred Stockton, Head of English Woodcote High School, and Ann Lovelace and Angela Allson for their permission to use *Ivory Man*.

NOTES TO TEACHERS

About the Play Scripts

Stepping Up is a set of four play scripts about Year Seven pupils which follows their progress throughout the year in their new secondary school. Whilst all the plays raise important issues, such as racism, friendship, loyalty, bullying and caring about others, they are not intended to be 'issue' plays as such. They are written in a light-hearted manner and are intended to be fun to read, or perform, and enjoyed by all. These play scripts are designed for classroom use and can also be used to equal effect in the Drama Studio. The Speaking and Listening and Writing activities, at the back of the book, are based on the requirements of the National Curriculum, Key Stage 3.

Activities

The authors' experience has shown that pupils' written work is of a significantly higher quality when based on oral activities directly linked to that written work. All activities, therefore, begin with Speaking and Listening and are followed by Writing.

Pupils should be encouraged to make notes on the Oral Activities performed by the rest of the class, so that they can choose to write about an activity which they have not prepared themselves. However, whether or not the activities are used in whole or in part, they are a valuable resource fulfilling the oral and written criteria of the National Curriculum, Key Stage 3, including the study of play scripts.

Help Notes

There are Help Notes at the back of the book. These make it possible for a variety of different activities, which reflect the full range of pupils' interests and abilities, to be going on in the classroom at the same time.

About the Authors

Each of the authors has extensive experience of teaching English and Drama in the secondary sector. Mollie Hemens is a former Head of Drama and Jane Liddiard, a former English teacher, is now a playwright.

First Day

Jane Liddiard

List of Characters

Pupils
Debbie
Karen
Gary
Rina
Mickey
Desmond
Daniel
Peter
Prefect 1
Prefect 2

Teachers
Ms Strange, English and Drama
Mrs Davies, Head of English
Mr Greenslade (Mr G.), Head of Year Seven
Miss McPherson (Miss McP.), P.T.

Parents
Mr Carrington (Mr C. – Debbie's Dad)
Gary's Nan
Mrs Greene (Gary's Mum)

FIRST DAY

Scene One

Characters: Debbie, Karen, Gary.

The first day of the new school year. Debbie, Karen and Gary are walking to school.

Gary How are you two feeling?

Debbie All right.

Karen A bit nervous. My stomach feels awful. What are the teachers like?

Gary OK, but a bit strict. There's lots of rules and they get really stressed about smoking.

Debbie Well, I don't smoke.

Gary Yah, bet you will soon.

Debbie No, I won't.

Gary Yes, you will. Everybody does.

Debbie I will not.

Gary Ooh, little Miss Goody-Goody.

Debbie belts him with her bag.

Debbie Shut up, you!

Gary (*laughing*) Ooh, that really hurt! I'll be injured for life. Bet my arm falls off tonight!

Karen I don't know how I'm going to find my way around our new school. It's so big.

Gary Have to run then, won't you?

Karen You're not allowed to run, stupid.

Gary Have to fly then.

Karen You're daft.

Gary Not half as daft as you are.

*She tries to thump him but he steps out of the way.
He grabs her bag and runs off laughing.*

Karen   Hey, give that back, Gary!

*She chases him to get her bag back. They each hold
on to the bag. Suddenly he lets go and she staggers
off the kerb. A passing car swerves and hoots its
horn.*

Karen   That was dangerous, Gary, you might have got us
killed!

Gary   OK, OK, keep your hair on, I didn't mean it.

Karen   Well, don't do it then.

Gary   Blimey, you're touchy this morning.

Debbie   She's nervous, that's all. Leave her alone.

*They walk along quietly for a while, each lost in
their own thoughts.*

Debbie   My Mum didn't half go on this morning. *'Debbie,
have you got this? Debbie, have you got that?' 'Yes,
Mum. Yes, Mum. Yes, Mum.'*

Gary   My Mum complained about the cost of the uniform.
She thinks these blazers are a right con. What's
wrong with a decent sweatshirt?

Debbie   Yes, and they're a horrible colour. Green. Yuk!

Gary   Sick bags!

They turn into the school road.

Gary   Here we are, the school gates.

Karen   Look at all those people!

Gary   It's all right, they aren't going to bite you. Wonder
how many times we'll have to walk through these
before we leave.

Debbie   Thousands, I bet.

Gary   The best part will be walking out of them again after
school. Yeah, can't wait.

Karen   You aren't even in yet.

Gary	Don't know why we have to go to school. It's a waste of time.
Karen	I like it.
Gary	What? There must be something wrong with you.
Debbie	Come on, you two, stop arguing and let's go in.
Gary	Wow, this is it!

Gary puts on a gangster voice

Fink-Face took a deep breath as he passed through those iron gates. The chains clinked and he looked at the tall, grey building. Prison here I come, he croaked.

Scene Two

Characters: Gary, Daniel, Debbie, Karen, Mickey, Prefect 1, Ms Strange.

7S's classroom at the first Registration. The bell has gone but Ms Strange, the form tutor, has not yet arrived. The Prefect is trying to keep the class in order.

Prefect 1	Shut up, you lot! You're making far too much noise. Oi, you at the back there, get off that bookshelf and sit down.

Something whizzes past the Prefect's ear.

Prefect 1	Who did that?

No one answers.

Come on, I said, who did that?

Daniel	Quick, give me another one and I'll do it this time.

Gary	Here you are then but be careful, the Prefect's watching.
Daniel	No problem! Watch this.

Daniel takes a paper pellet and pings it at the Prefect, who is hit on the shoulder.

Prefect 1	Right, that's it! Who did that?

Mickey points to Daniel.

Mickey	He did.
Daniel	No, I didn't. He's lying. I didn't, did I, Gary?
Gary	Nah, no chance. He's not a good enough shot.

He indicates Mickey.

He's just trying to get us into trouble. Probably did it himself.

Mickey	I did not, liar!

Gary stands up.

Gary	Who are you calling a liar?

Mickey gets up.

Mickey	Don't kid yourself.
Prefect 1	All right, you two, that's enough. Sit down, both of you, and shut up, and that goes for all of you!

Nobody takes any notice. The noise goes on.

Daniel speaks to Mickey.

Daniel	You'd better watch it.
Gary	Yeah, that's the last time you grass us up, mate.
Mickey	Oh, yeah? You don't scare me, hard man.
Gary	No?
Mickey	No!
Karen	This noise is awful. I hope it's not going to be like this all the time.
Debbie	It's only because there's no teacher here. Fancy

being late on our first day!

Karen Do you think we'll be allowed to sit together?

Debbie Don't know. Gary, do you know if we'll be allowed to sit next to who we like?

Gary No chance. It's alphabetical.

Karen Gary!

Gary Well, I'm only telling the truth.

Debbie I hope we don't have to sit next to any boys. I'd hate that.

Gary What's wrong with boys?

Debbie What's right with them? They're noisy and silly and smelly.

Gary Charming, I'm sure.

Daniel Ah, don't take any notice. Girls aren't much better. They're wimps and wet and whingers.

Debbie No, we're not.

Gary Yes, you are. You're pathetic.

Debbie Thought you were meant to be my friend.

Karen Stop it, you two. I'm feeling sick.

Daniel Put your head down. Do you want me to get the waste paper bin?

Karen No, I'll be all right.

Karen puts her head down on the desk. The Prefect sees this and comes over.

Prefect 1 Is she all right?

Debbie She's feeling sick.

Prefect 1 Do you want to take her to the toilets?

Debbie No, I don't think she will be sick. She'll be OK in a minute, thanks.

Prefect 1 Right.

The Prefect walks back to the desk and is hit on the back by a pellet but does not notice this time. Gary and Daniel laugh. Suddenly the door is flung open and Ms Strange stands there glaring at everybody. A pellet hits the wall near the door. She is not pleased. Gradually the noise dies away and there is silence. Ten minutes later the class is rearranged into alphabetical order. Debbie is next to Emma, Karen next to Rina, Gary next to Daniel, and Mickey next to Desmond. The Register has been taken.

Ms Strange Good. That didn't take long, did it?

Mickey gets up.

Excuse me, Michael, where are you going?

Mickey To have a word with my mate. You've put him all over the other side and stuck me with some stupid geezer I don't know.

Ms Strange Sit down, please.

Mickey What?

Prefect 1 Sit down, Parry. You heard.

Mickey sits down reluctantly.

Mickey Can't even talk to your mates in this school.

Ms Strange This is 'Big School', young man, and we do not wander all over the classroom without asking permission first.

Mickey If that's all you want, can I have a word with Carl? Thanks.

Mickey gets up. The Prefect pushes him back.

Here, watch it! You're not allowed to do that.

Ms Strange Sit down, Michael. It's not convenient for you to talk to your friend at the moment.

Mickey That's not fair. It's stupid.

Ms Strange Right, listen everybody. I expect you all to be here on time each day. No lurking around the back of the bike sheds for a quick cigarette. If I'm delayed for some reason, the Prefect will take the Register and you will behave whilst it's being done.

Desmond springs up angrily.

Desmond   Ow! Get off!

Ms Strange   What's going on?

Desmond   He's punching me, Miss.

Mickey   He started it.

Desmond   I did not, you did. You scribbled on my book.

Mickey   Liar!

Ms Strange   Enough, both of you, or I will move you.

Mickey   Don't want to sit with him, anyway. He smells.

Desmond   Not as much as you do.

Mickey   Say that again and I'll floor you.

Ms Strange   That's enough. Michael, you will stand outside if there's any more of this.

Mickey   That's not fair. You're picking on me. My Dad'll make a complaint against you.

Ms Strange ignores him.

Ms Strange   Right, class, let's get down to business.

Scene Three

Characters: Debbie, Karen, Rina, Gary, Mickey.

It is first break. Debbie, Karen, Rina, and Gary are in the playground.

Rina speaks to Karen

Rina   You don't mind having to sit next to me, do you?

Karen   No, why should I?

Rina   I thought Debbie was your best friend.

Karen She is but it doesn't really matter. I can sit next to her in lessons.

Gary rushes up.

Gary Hey, girls, what a morning! All that stuff we were given. I'll never remember half of it.

Debbie You don't have to remember it. That's why we had to write it down.

She takes a chocolate bar out of her pocket and starts to eat it.

Gary Never done so much writing in all my life. Could have written my biography.

Karen Autobiography.

Gary Yeah, one of them as well. Give us a bit of that Mars, Debs.

Debbie You should have your own.

Gary I prefer somebody else's. Nah, only joking.

Debbie holds it away from him.

Aw, come on, only a small bit. I'm starving.

Debbie hands him the chocolate.

Debbie OK, but don't take the lot.

Gary Thanks, promise I won't.

Gary breaks off a piece and hands it back.

Our new teacher's all right, isn't she? But if that Mickey comes anywhere near me I'll take him out. He's a right divvy.

Karen I hope he isn't going to be like that all the time.

Gary Don't worry, girls, I'll sort him out for you.

Debbie We can manage by ourselves, thanks.

Gary Ooh, tough!

Gary speaks to Rina.

Don't you ever speak?

Rina   When there's something to say, yes.

Gary   Right, seems like you don't need a bloke around so I'm off.

He shouts.

Oi, Daniel!

He runs off.

Watcher, mate!

Rina   Wait, I'm sorry. I didn't mean to upset him.

Karen   Don't worry. He's OK most of the time, just fancies himself a bit, that's all. He's got a brother in Year Nine and he thinks that makes him big.

Rina   I've got a sister in the Sixth Form, Year Twelve.

Karen   She must be a lot older than you.

Rina   Yes, but I've got a brother as well. He's sixteen. He's at a different school.

She hesitates and then changes the subject very quickly.

I was really frightened about coming this morning, weren't you?

Karen   Yes, I couldn't stop shaking.

Debbie I was up and dressed at a quarter past seven. My Mum couldn't believe it. I couldn't get up at all in the holidays.

Karen   Nor me.

Debbie What's happening after break?

Rina   The rest of the school have normal lessons whilst we have an Assembly and then get shown round the school.

Debbie Oh yes, I forgot. Gary's right, there *is* too much to remember.

A bell rings.

Debbie That's the end of break. We'd better go in.

They move off but as they do so Mickey rushes past and collides with Rina.

Mickey	Here, watch where you're going, you stupid git!
Rina	You bumped into me.
Mickey	Oh yeah, who says so?
Karen	We do because we saw you do it.
Mickey	Who's asking you, Four-Eyes? I was talking to the Paki here.
Rina	I'm not Pakistani. I'm British. I was born here.
Mickey	Bet your old man and old girl wasn't.
Rina	No, so what?
Mickey	So, you're a Paki like I said.
Rina	I'm not. My parents are not from Pakistan. They're from India, actually.

Mickey laughs and makes Red Indian whoops.

Mickey	Your old man got a sweet shop, has he? Bet he has. All your lot have. Coming over here taking all our shops.
Rina	No, he's an accountant.
Mickey	What's that then? Counts the sweets, does he?
Karen	You're so ignorant.
Mickey	Quiet, Hog-Face, nobody's asking you.
Debbie	You leave her alone, and Rina. They haven't done anything to you.
Mickey	Who's asking you, Skinny-Ribs? You're just a skellington. What are you, annalectic or something?
Debbie	What?
Karen	He means anorexic.
Mickey	Skelly-Elly.

He jabs his finger in Rina's face.

Just watch yourself, Paki. You won't always have these two silly moos sticking up for you.

Karen   Will you get out of our way! We want to go in. The bell's gone.

Mickey   Yah, stupid all of you.

He speaks to Rina.

But you'd better watch it. I'll be waiting for you after school, then I'll get you.

He jeers at them and runs off. Rina is crying. Karen puts an arm round her shoulder.

Karen   It's all right, Rina, he's gone now.

Debbie   Yes, don't get upset over him. He's not worth bothering about.

Rina   Do you think he really will wait for me after school?

Karen   I don't know, but if you walk home with us and Gary you should be OK. Where do you live?

Rina   Cranleigh Avenue.

Karen   Great, that's on our way.

Debbie   We'll tell Miss about him. He's not allowed to talk to us like that.

Rina   Will she do anything?

Karen   Yes. That boy isn't allowed to behave like that. She told us to tell her if it happened.

Debbie   Come on, let's go in or we'll be late!

Scene Four

Characters: Debbie, Karen, Rina, Gary, Prefect 2.

The school Dining Hall is packed with pupils and teachers. Debbie and the others are having lunch together.

Debbie Don't like these chips.

Gary Give them to me if you don't like them.

He reaches for her chips. She smacks his hand with her fork.

Debbie Get off! I didn't say you could have them. I only said I didn't like them.

Gary If you don't like them give them to me.

Karen You're a dustbin, Gary, a disgusting dustbin.

Gary Yeah, that's me. Gary The Disgusting Dustbin. Give me all the food you don't want and I'll gobble it up. Gobble, gobble, gobble. Yum, yum, yum.

He reaches for her chips again but she moves her plate out of the way and his arm falls in the ketchup on his own plate.

Debbie Get off!

Gary Now look what you've made me do.

Karen Why don't you eat something decent, anyway?

Gary sucks at the ketchup on his sleeve.

Gary What, like that stuff you're eating?

Karen What's wrong with it?

Gary There's no chips for a start.

Karen I don't eat chips.

Gary Don't eat chips? Everyone eats chips!

Karen My Mum says they're bad for me. Too much fat and starch.

Gary	*'Too much fat and starch.'* Your Mum must be crazy. Chips are great, and what's that cakky stuff in the bottom of your lunchbox?
Karen	Lentils.
Gary	Ugh, gross! Looks like dog sick.
Debbie	Shut up, Gary, you're putting me off my dinner.
Gary	Well, she's putting me off mine. Look at that muck in her lunch box. Is her Mum a health freak, or what?
Karen	She's not a freak but she doesn't let me eat rubbish like you eat.
Gary	This is lovely grub. What do you mean?
Karen	We're vegetarians.
Gary	Don't eat meat? You don't know what you're missing.
Rina	It's what you're used to, Gary. We don't eat meat either.
Karen	We shouldn't be killing animals just so we can eat them. What about all those poor calves chained up in crates for the whole of their lives? It's cruel.
Gary	They're only animals. They can't feel nothing.
Karen	Of course they can!
Debbie	I don't mind eating meat but Mum always buys free-range eggs.
Gary	All right if you can afford all that fancy stuff.
Debbie	My uncle has a farm in Cornwall. He's got dairy cattle – you know, for milk – but they're well looked after.
Karen	What about the calves who get sent off for slaughter?
Debbie	I don't know. I only know that my uncle wouldn't do anything nasty to his animals. That would be daft. They have to live off that farm.
Gary	Has he had a bomb sent through the post from the animal crazies?

Debbie	(*Alarmed*) I don't know. Why?
Rina	Gary, you shouldn't be saying things like that! Of course he hasn't, Debbie, or you would have heard.
Gary	Animal Rights people can get a bit silly sometimes though, can't they? Threatening people with bombs and so on.
Karen	That's because no one will do anything about it unless you get serious.
Debbie	I care about animals.
Karen	Yes, but that's not enough, just saying it. You've got to do something.
Gary	It's got nothing to do with me. I can't help what the farmers do. They've got to make a living, haven't they? I've got to eat. And our teacher in the Juniors said that if all the hens were free range they'd need a place the size of Wales to live in. Chips and beans are OK, aren't they? Though I bet you're going to say that it's cruel to chop potatoes up into little pieces and throw them into boiling hot fat. Bet you belong to the NSPCC. The National Society For the Prevention of Cruelty to Chips!
Karen	You're really silly sometimes.
Gary	No, come on, what's wrong with them then?
Karen	Fat and starch and monosodium glutamate.
Gary	*Monosode-what?* Don't you swear at me. You're unbelievable, you are, and another thing, didn't you know that eating too much lettuce makes you pregnant?
	The girls roar with laughter.
Debbie	Don't be stupid, Gary.
Gary	It's true, I swear it.
Rina	Science with you is going to be a laugh.
	Karen puts on a teacher's voice.
Karen	Gary's experiment today will be on a pregnant lettuce!

They laugh again.

Rina It's huge in here, isn't it? Hope we don't have to wait ages to get our lunch tomorrow.

Debbie Yes, the teachers and seniors come straight in and go right up to the counter and push everybody out of the way.

Gary Yeah, it's not fair. Still, who'd want to be a teacher?

Debbie Yeah, who'd want to teach people like you?

Karen My mother's a teacher. Well, lecturer actually, at the local college.

Gary That explains why she gives you all that stuff to eat if she's a lecherer. Bet she's trying to poison you.

Karen Gary!

Gary Only joking.

Rina is looking very pale.

You all right, Rina?

Rina Yes, why?

Gary You've gone all funny looking. What's the matter?

Rina I just saw that boy again, Mickey Parry. He walked right by and looked straight at me.

Gary What you bothered about him for? Don't worry, girls, he won't come near you when I'm around. I make ten of him.

Debbie Listen to Rambo. I bet that Mickey's getting really scared already.

Gary He will do when me and my mates have finished duffing him up.

Rina No, Gary, you're not to get yourself into any trouble for my sake. You know the rules about fighting. Ms Strange is going to talk to him this lunchtime.

Gary *Talk* to him! Fat lot of good that will do.

He mimics Ms Strange.

Now, look here, young man, this will not do. It's very

naughty, you know, to go pushing girls around and being ever so unkind to poor little Rina.

They fall about laughing. Prefect 2 shouts from further up the table.

Prefect 2 Oi, you lot, shut up!

Gary Charming, I must say.

They try to stop laughing but Gary starts making faces and they laugh again.

The Prefect speaks to Gary.

Prefect 2 Did you say something?

Gary Me? Nah, nothing.

Prefect 2 Because if you did, I'll have you.

Gary I didn't, honest, did I, girls?

The three girls try not to laugh.

All Three No.

Prefect 2 Just remember I've got your card marked, you divvy.

Gary Ooh, we've got a right card here.

Prefect 2 OK, that does it –

The Prefect gets up and Gary quickly ducks under the table.

Gary I think I'd better go, girls. I've just remembered I've got to play football with Daniel. I'd invite you as well, only girls ...

Karen (*interrupting*) Can't play football?

Gary No, did I say that? Did I say girls can't play football?

Debbie No.

Gary pops his head up.

Gary All I'm saying is, girls can't play football.

He dives under the table again as the Prefect begins to move and crawls to the top end where he escapes and makes a quick exit.

Karen shouts after him.

Karen Don't play too much football, Gary. It might make you pregnant!

They laugh loudly again. The Prefect comes over to them.

The Prefect speaks to Karen.

Prefect 2 I thought I told you lot to shut up. And what are you doing eating a packed lunch with the hot dinners? You should be on a packed lunch table over there.

Karen I'm sorry, I didn't know.

Prefect 2 Well you do now. Come on, move.

Rina Oh, please let her stay just for today. We've nearly finished.

Debbie Please.

Prefect 2 OK, but tomorrow she's on the right tables – and don't keep making so much noise or I'll make the whole lot of you move to separate tables.

Debbie Yes, we promise.

The Prefect goes away but the giggles threaten to break out again and they have to put their heads down to try to suppress them.

Debbie Gary was ever so funny at our last school. He was always making us laugh. The teachers used to get fed up with him because he could never keep still or sit quietly.

Rina Did he get into a lot of trouble?

Debbie No, he never got into any. The teachers told him off a lot but he never got sent to the Head or anything.

Rina Some people are lucky like that. They always manage to stay out of trouble somehow. I wish my brother ...

She stops suddenly.

Debbie You wish your brother what?

Rina	Oh, nothing. Was just like Gary, I suppose.
Debbie	You wouldn't want a brother like Gary, would you? Well, I wouldn't.
Rina	I think he's all right, actually.
Karen	Come on, finish up. We've got to get to the Art Studio by half-past if we're going to join the Art Club.

Scene Five

Characters: Ms Strange, Mickey, Mrs Davies.

Mickey is seeing Ms Strange in her classroom at lunchtime.

Ms Strange	Sit down, Mickey.
	Mickey sits on the edge of a desk.
	No, not on the desk. On a chair.
	She points to a chair in front of her desk. He sits down making a lot of noise.
Ms Strange	You are in very serious trouble indeed. You have behaved in a very offensive manner towards Rina Gupta.
Mickey	She said she was British. She's a liar. She ain't.
Ms Strange	She is by birth and nationality. She was born in this country just like you were.
Mickey	She's a Paki.
Ms Strange	We don't use that term here, Mickey. It's offensive. As a matter of fact, Rina's family are from India.
Mickey	It's all the same.
Ms Strange	No, it isn't. It's like referring to Scottish, or Irish, or

	Welsh people as English. How would you like that?
Mickey	Wouldn't bother me.
Ms Strange	Well, it bothers me and it bothers Rina, and this school will not allow it. Why did you single out Rina?
Mickey	I didn't. She bashed into me. She nearly knocked me flying.
Ms Strange	According to Karen and Debbie it was you who knocked into Rina.
Mickey	They're just backing up their friend.
Ms Strange	But you did say unpleasant and unacceptable things to all three of them.
Mickey	Four-Eyes is all right. What's wrong with that? She wears glasses, doesn't she?
Ms Strange	Yes, she does but there is no need to comment on it.
Mickey	Everybody says it and one of them is a skellington, a right skinny-ribs.
Ms Strange	That does not give you the right to be nasty and rude about them.
Mickey	Why are you picking on me? I haven't done nothing. It's not fair.

Mrs Davies walks in briskly.

Ms Strange	Stand up for Mrs Davies.

Mickey stands up very reluctantly.

Mrs Davies	Sit down, lad.
Mickey	Stand up. Sit down. What next?
Mrs Davies	Don't dare speak to me like that, Parry!
Ms Strange	I don't think he appreciates how serious this is.
Mrs Davies	Doesn't he? Well, Mr Greenslade and I will soon change all that. Right, Parry, up. Wait outside this room.
Mickey	Yes, Miss.

Mrs Davies	*Mrs Davies* to you.
Mickey	Yes, Mrs Davies.
Mrs Davies	Go on then. Out!

He scuttles out, closing the door quietly after him.

Ms Strange	How do you do it? He was so rude to me!
Mrs Davies	Years of practice. When you're an old hag like me they don't try it on. So, how did it go?
Ms Strange	Not very well. There's something wrong here, Ann. He's rude and says he doesn't care if he's suspended but I think he does. Something wrong at home, perhaps?
Mrs Davies	Quite possible. I'd better go and see what Frank can get out of him.

Scene Six

Characters: Mrs Davies, Mr Greenslade, Mickey.

Mr Greenslade is in his office with Mrs Davies. Mickey is in the corridor.

Mr G.	What a lad! What's up with him, do you reckon?
Mrs Davies	Don't know, can't work it out, Frank. The reports from his last school are all fine. Working well. No problems.
Mr G.	So what's happened to turn him in the holidays?
Mrs Davies	Perhaps it's something to do with home.
Mr G.	OK, let's have him in and try to find out what's up.

He goes to the door and calls Mickey in. Mickey comes in quickly.

Mr G.   Stand there in front of my desk and don't move
               unless I tell you.

               Mickey goes to the desk.

Mickey   No, Sir.

Mr G.   Mrs Davies, here, tells me that you've been accused
               of racist and abusive behaviour towards three girls
               in your class and that you've been rude and insolent
               to your teacher. You've only been in this school five
               minutes. I tell you, Parry, I rue the day they ever got
               rid of corporal punishment. Know what that is?

Mickey   Yes, Sir. It's hitting kids, Sir.

Mr G.   That's it, son. You've got it. In my younger days you
               could give a lad a right thumping. *They* knew where
               they were. *You* knew where you were. And that was
               that. But nowadays you can't even look at them
               without them saying. *'I'll get my Dad down here to
               you. We'll sue you for every penny you've got.'*

Mickey   Yes, Sir.

Mr G.   The point is, lad, what's up with you? It seems you
               were a paragon of virtue in your last school.

Mickey   What, Sir?

Mrs Davies Mr Greenslade means, Mickey, that you did very
               well at your other school so why are you behaving
               so badly here?

               *He does not answer. Mr Greenslade gets up angrily
               and Mickey steps back.*

Mr G.   Come on, Parry, stop messing us about!

Mrs Davies (*gently*) Something has happened, hasn't it? To
               make you so unhappy at the moment. (*Pause.*) You
               can tell us, you know. We're here to help you, not
               just to punish you.

               *Mickey is near to tears. He wants to say but can't.
               He scrambles away and runs to the door but
               Mr Greenslade heads him off and grabs hold of him.*

Mickey   Get off me, get off! Let me go!

Mr G.   Steady, lad, calm down. You're going nowhere so you might as well settle down.

Mrs Davies   Come on, Mickey, Mr Greenslade is only trying to stop you for your own good. You don't want the other pupils to see you like this, do you?

Mickey mumbles through his tears.

Mickey   No.

Mickey stops struggling and Mr Greenslade lets him sit down.

You're all the same, always telling me what to do all the time. You're worse than my Mum and Dad!

Mrs Davies   Has this got something to do with your parents?

Mickey nods.

Have they stopped you from seeing your friends?

Mickey   No.

Mrs Davies   Going out at night?

Mickey   No.

Mr G.   Listen, lad, we're not here to play twenty questions. Tell us.

Mickey   It's not fair! They won't even let me see Nan and Gramps just because they've had a row with them. Mum and Dad won't even speak to them now and they won't let me go and see them but I will, I'll run away and I won't come back and that'll serve them right!

Mr G.   OK, Parry, calm down. Let's see if we can get this sorted. We're having your parents in to discuss this morning's little episode so we can ask them about this as well. But we can't have you carrying on like this morning. You know how serious that is?

Mickey   Yes, Sir.

Mr G.   Good, because whatever else happens that has to be sorted. Right?

Mickey   Yes, Sir, I'm really sorry, Sir.

Mr G.   Good, that's a step in the right direction but your next apology should be to those girls.

Mickey   Yes, Sir.

Scene Seven

Characters: Ms Strange, Peter, Desmond, Gary.

It is afternoon Registration. 7S is listening quietly to Ms Strange.

Ms Strange   Good, that's the Register taken care of. Does anyone know where the missing boys are?

Gary   No, Miss, 'spect they're looking for this classroom – in another school!

Ms Strange   Thank you, Gary, for those helpful comments.

The door opens and Desmond and Peter come in sheepishly. They go up to Ms Strange's desk but are too worried to speak.

Ms Strange   Well? (*Pause*) Just tell me, boys, I'm not going to bite your heads off.

Desmond   Ah ... um ... sorry, Miss, but we didn't um ... get our lunch until the bell went.

Ms Strange   How on earth did that happen? All Year Sevens were meant to be in the first sitting today.

Desmond   We know, Miss, but the prefects said there were too many in the queue so we had to wait till the end.

Gary   It's true, Miss, all the seniors and all the teachers pushed in and took our places, and all the grub went, and –

Ms Strange	Thank you, Gary. I see, the usual Kingsley Vale shambles. OK, boys, not to worry this time. It obviously wasn't your fault. Did you manage to get something to eat?
Desmond	There wasn't much left but we had something.
Gary	Lentils and lettuce, Miss. They'll get pregnant!

The class erupts in laughter.

Ms Strange is not amused.

Ms Strange	Gary, I really must insist that you don't keep interrupting in this way.
Gary	OK, Miss, I won't say a single word.
Ms Strange	Good. We'll see how long it lasts. Right, boys, sit down. I've something very important to say. A boy in this class was involved in a very serious incident this morning.
Desmond	Who, Miss?
Gary	That berk Parry, who else? Oops, sorry, Miss.
Desmond	What did he do?
Gary	He had a go at my friends. I'll do him for that. Oops, sorry, Miss.
Ms Strange	He made racist remarks to Rina.
Desmond	What about?

Ms Strange tries to be patient.

Ms Strange	I'm not going to go into details but suffice to say that we do not make remarks about other people's appearance, or figure, or race. This school will not tolerate such behaviour. It is categorically against the school rules and you can expect to be severely punished for such behaviour. Normally, it's suspension –
Gary	Oh, great, is he going home?
Ms Strange	Not this time because it's his first day but normally, yes.

Gary	Cor, fix!

The class breaks out into lots of talking.

Ms Strange	Settle down, please. So, be warned. When you go home tonight have a good look at the School Rules booklet. Have you all got a copy?
All	Yes, Miss.
Peter	No, Miss.
Ms Strange	Peter De Souza, isn't it?
Peter	Yes, Miss.
Ms Strange	See me at the end of the lesson and I'll give you a copy. Have you all got your Year Seven pack?
All	Yes, Miss.
Peter	No, Miss.
Gary	What a wally!
Ms Strange	Gary, when I want your comments I'll ask for them.
Gary	Sorry, Miss, my lips are sealed.
Ms Strange	Sewn up would be better. Peter, you were here this morning, weren't you?
Peter	Yes, Miss, I think so.
Desmond	He was, Miss.
Ms Strange	Then how did you manage to miss the hand outs?
Peter	Don't know, Miss.
Desmond	He was like this at our last school, Miss, and he's always getting lost.
Ms Strange	A bit of a walking disaster by the looks of things. Well, Peter, you will have to open the top of that empty head of yours each morning and pop your brain inside.
Gary	You're good at remembering names, Miss.
Ms Strange	Yes, Gary, and I always remember the awkward ones first.
Desmond	Yah, sussed.
Gary	Watch it.

Ms Strange	Don't forget, you have English here in this room last lesson of the day with me.

They all moan but don't really mean it. The bell rings and everybody starts to pack up. They all file out including Peter. Ms Strange sees him and calls him back.

Ms Strange	Peter.
Peter	Yes, Miss.
Ms Strange	I thought you were meant to stay behind and see me.
Peter	Oh, yes, I forgot.

Desmond waits too. Ms Strange hands Peter a Year Seven pack and the School Rules.

Ms Strange	Put these in your bag and keep them safely.

He looks around for his bag. Desmond fetches it and gives it to him.

Ms Strange	You do know where you're going this afternoon, don't you?
Peter	Yes, Miss, Science –
Ms Strange	I don't believe this. No, it's Art first. Desmond, keep with him and make sure he gets to all his lessons.
Desmond	Don't worry, Miss, I'll see he's all right.
Ms Strange	Thank you, Desmond. Now off you go or you'll be late and Mr Bourne won't like that one little bit.

They go. Ms Strange gives a little scream.

Ms Strange	Something tells me I'm back!

Scene Eight

Characters: Mrs Davies, Desmond, Gary, Peter.

Mrs Davies is hurrying to her sixth form lesson. On her way she sees Desmond and Gary lurking in the corridor.

Mrs Davies Boys, where are you supposed to be?

Desmond Art, but we're looking for a boy in 7S, our class, Miss.

Mrs Davies *Mrs Davies*, not Miss. Who's missing?

Gary Peter De Souza, Miss – er Mrs Davies. He's a right wally. He doesn't know what time of day it is.

Mrs Davies Is it likely that he's left the building?

Desmond No, Mrs Davies, he likes school. He's just useless at finding places.

Gary He was meant to hold on to Peter. Ms Strange told him.

Desmond It wasn't my fault. The corridor was packed and everyone was pushing and shoving and we got lost in the crush.

Mrs Davies Have you any idea where he's likely to be?

Desmond No. Once at our old school he was found locked in the cleaner's broom cupboard.

Gary Divvy!

Mrs Davies Have you checked the toilets?

Desmond Yes.

Gary sees Peter wandering along the corridor looking into classrooms.

Gary Oh, no, here he comes!

Desmond Peter, where have you been, man?

Peter I went to Science but I could see she had another class in there.

Desmond That's because we've got Art now.

Mrs Davies I think enough time's been wasted already, boys. Run along now.

Gary Come on, mate, we'll look after you.

They both take hold of Peter and hurry off.

Scene Nine

Characters: Ms Strange, Mrs Davies, Gary, Desmond, Karen, Daniel, Miss McPherson.

It is the last but one lesson of the afternoon. Ms Strange and Mrs Davies are walking along the corridor. It is Ms Strange's free period.

Ms Strange I tell you, Ann, I've had an absolutely awful day. I'm so glad to have a free period now before 7S descend on me yet again.

Mrs Davies I shouldn't speak too soon.

Ms Strange Oh no, I don't believe this! De Souza can't be lost again.

Mrs Davies I should brace yourself, Catherine. It looks like the whole class. Sorry but I'm going to have to leave you to sort this one out. I've got a Year Ten group. I'm already late and they're probably rioting by now.

Mrs Davies goes. 7S straggle towards Ms Strange excitedly.

Ms Strange What on earth are you doing here? I thought you had Science.

Desmond We did, Miss, but when we got there the teacher already had a class and he told us to go away.

Desmond	Why did they send us to the wrong place, Miss?
Ms Strange	It wasn't deliberate, Desmond. The computer crashed a few days ago and the timetable isn't properly sorted out yet. It would have to be my class during my one and only free period, wouldn't it?
Gary	Yeah, are you always this lucky, Miss?
Karen	Gary!
Ms Strange	Yes, Gary, always. Haven't I got you to prove it?
Gary	I think Miss likes me.
Karen	Gary!
Ms Strange	OK, everybody, listen. I'm going to take you along to the Hall for now. Gary, I want you to have a look in this block and see if there is an empty classroom anywhere. Then come back to the Hall.
Gary	Yeah!

Gary runs off.

Ms Strange	Walk, don't run. Stop talking, all of you.

She waits.

That's better. Make a line in pairs. Don't push, there's room for all of you. Come on, you people at the back, let's have some order.

When they get to the Hall Miss McPherson is taking a dance class. The girls are in gym kit or leotards and are dancing with free expression, arms waving. Music is playing loudly. Mrs McPherson speaks with a Scottish accent.

Miss McP.	And skip and hop and stop and arms above your heads, and wave gently, and sway. Remember you're trees in a gentle breeze. That's good. Keep it going.
Daniel	Oh, no, not cissy old dancing!
Karen	Ssh.
Daniel	Ssh yourself.

Miss McPherson switches off her music with a flourish of great irritation and goes over to Ms Strange.

Miss McP. Ms Strange, what are all these pupils doing here?

Ms Strange There's been a mix-up in the timetable.

Miss McP. That's hardly my problem. I am timetabled to have a lesson in here. I can't have these hooligans running about all over the place.

Ms Strange They are not hooligans, Miss McPherson. They are a little excited, that's all. I'm off to find the Deputy Head but I can hardly take all thirty children with me, can I?

Miss McP. (*grudgingly*) I suppose not but they'd better behave themselves.

Ms Strange I'm sure they will. Thank you so much for your help.

Gary comes rushing in.

Miss McP. Walk, boy, don't run!

Gary speaks to Ms Strange.

Gary Sorry, Miss. No classrooms free, Miss. There's a teacher in every one of them, and I looked in all the other classrooms on my way back.

Ms Strange Thank you, Gary. OK, everybody, listen carefully. Miss McPherson has a dance lesson going on in here so what I want you to do is to keep to this corner of the Hall, sit down and get on with something quietly.

Daniel Like what, Miss?

Ms Strange Like anything – reading, homework – anything so long as you don't disturb Miss McPherson. I am going to go and see if I can find someone to sort this out.

She goes. Miss McPherson is not too pleased. She switches on her cassette of music and starts up her class again.

Daniel	This music's rubbish. *Bagpipes!*
Karen	They're not bagpipes, they're flutes. It's Debussy's …
Daniel	Yes, all right, Miss Know-It-All. What they need is a bit of rave.
Desmond	Yeah, man.
Daniel	And look at them girls dancing about like a load of stupid butterflies.

He stands up and mimics their dancing. Several of the others are laughing.

Daniel	Ooh, I'm a tree. I'm a butterfly.

Miss McPherson speaks to Daniel.

Miss McP.	You, boy, what do you think you are doing?
Daniel	I'm joining in, Miss. It's such fun. Do you think I'm any good?
Miss McP.	Don't be insolent, boy. Sit down!

Daniel sits down, still laughing, and deliberately falls on top of Desmond who shoves him off.

Desmond	Get off me, Smith.
Daniel	Do you think I'll make a ballet dancer? In my tights? Ooh, tight tights!
Karen	You're so childish.
Daniel	Who are you talking to? It's none of your business, Posh-Face.
Karen	You're not allowed to call people names.
Daniel	I'm not calling you names, I'm telling the truth.

He and some other boys laugh.

Gary	Leave her alone, Smith, or I'll rearrange your face and call you Ugly-Mug.
Daniel	All right, Greene, keep your hair on.

The dancing continues. Ms Strange does not return and some of the pupils get restless and start wandering about. Two of them go on to the stage and some others bat the window curtains about.

Miss McP. Come down off that stage, you two, and will you boys please stop swinging on that curtain. You'll have the whole lot down on top of you. Oh dear, oh dear, this is chaos!

Daniel smiles at a girl and winks.

Daniel Perhaps we can join in with the dancing. Bet some of you girls would like us as partners.

Gary Yeah, I'll be an elf and Smith can be a fairy.

Daniel Watch it, you!

While Miss McPherson isn't looking Daniel grabs one of the girls, who laughs and dances with him.

Desmond Get you, Smith! Right on, man.

Gary Woo!

Karen You boys are so stupid sometimes.

Daniel gives his partner another twirl but it is so fast that she falls over.

Miss McPherson speaks desperately to Daniel.

Miss McP. Will you *please* leave my girls alone and sit down and be quiet!

Daniel sees Ms Strange returning so he quickly scuttles to his place and sits down innocently.

Miss McP. Ms Strange, thank heavens you're back. I don't think I can cope with these pupils any longer. Will you boys please leave that piano alone! Oh dear, oh dear.

Ms Strange I'm sorry about this, Miss McPherson, but I can't find the Deputy Head and the Head's in a meeting, and the Head of Year is talking to some parents.

The girl Daniel was dancing with goes over to talk to him.

Gary That's OK, Miss, we'll all go home early.

Ms Strange	Nice though that may sound, Gary, I'm afraid you can't.
Miss McP.	Oh dear, what are we going to do now?
Ms Strange	Don't worry, I've decided to take them to the Library.
Gary	Cool!
Miss McP.	Thank goodness for that. Right, girls, just rest for a moment. This class is about to leave. Donna, will you come away from that boy and join the other girls.
Ms Strange	Right, everybody, pack up your things and let's go.

They pick up their bags and go over to the Hall door. Daniel catches his foot in Miss McPherson's radio-cassette lead, pulling it out. The music stops.

Miss McP.	Oh my goodness. Oh dear, now what I am I going to do?
Gary	You just put it back in again, Miss. It's simple. Here, I'll do it for you.

Gary puts the connector lead back into the radio.

Miss McP.	Thank you. What a clever boy.
Daniel	Creep.
Ms Strange	Come along, 7S, we're going to the Library.

They all cheer and troop out. Miss McPherson nearly faints with relief.

Scene Ten

Characters: Debbie, Karen, Gary, Rina, Daniel.

Debbie, Karen, Rina and Gary are walking home at the end of the first day at their new school.

Gary Well, girls, what do you think of your first day? Anyone ready to bunk off yet?

Debbie Don't be daft, Gary, we haven't been there five minutes.

Rina The Art Room's great and there's an Art Club.

Karen The Music Studio's really good, too. I can't wait to start my flute lessons again.

Gary *Flute?* You don't want to play the mouldy old flute. You want to play the electric guitar. Fantastic!

He plays an imaginary guitar.

Dah, dah-dah, dah, dah. Reeeow!!

Debbie What a racket.

Gary It's not a racquet, it's a guitar. Joe Satriani. Steve Vai. Guns 'N Roses. Metallica.

Rina I play the flute too.

Karen Great, we'll be able to practise together. We might even be in the school orchestra.

Rina Yes, that would be nice. It's Music Club on Friday. Will you come with me?

Karen Yes, of course. This is great, Rina.

Gary You two'll be getting married next.

Debbie You're only jealous.

Gary What, of a couple of silly old gir – I mean flutes. Bass guitar! Playing in a rock band! That's what I want.

Rina Well, perhaps you'll be able to, Gary. There are several bands at the school.

Gary   Cor, cool. Thanks, Rina. At least there are some
decent people around here – which is more than I
can say for some.

*He looks straight at Debbie. She sticks her tongue
out at him but he ignores her.*

Gary   Do you feel better now, Rina, about that Mickey
idiot?

Rina   Oh, yes. Mrs Davies says it's all sorted out.

Karen   Good. Horrible bullies like him deserve all they get.

Gary   He's probably all right really.

Karen   Gary, how can you say that when you know what he
did?

Gary   Nah, listen, right, he was just trying to be big, right,
because he feels small.

Debbie   I hate him. I hope you're not going to be friends
with him, Gary.

Gary   I'm only telling you what I think. Don't worry, Debs,
I'll keep him away.

Debbie   Ooh, thanks, Tarzan.

Gary   Yeah, Tarzan.

*He makes Tarzan noises and beats his chest, then
grabs hold of Debbie.*

You Jane, me Tarzan. Ooh, ooh-oh, ooh-oh!

Debbie   Get off, Gary!

*Daniel passes by on his bike. He slows down and
cycles alongside them.*

Daniel   Walking home with me?

Gary   No, I'm with Rina and them.

Daniel   Rather be with girls? You're crazy, mate. Yeah, that's
'cos you want to be one.

Gary starts after Daniel but he cycles off shouting.

Daniel   Girlie, girlie Gary. Girlie, girlie Gary.

Gary   I'll get you for that, Daniel Smith.

Rina   Don't take any notice, Gary. He's not worth it.

Gary   I'll catch up with him later. Hey, it was a right laugh this afternoon. That Miss McPersil, or whatever her name was, didn't half go on.

He mimics her Scottish accent.

'Och, get doon off that stage and stop claiming on those currtanes. Oooh, ma nerrves! Oh dear, oh dear.' And Ms Strange wasn't too happy either.

He mimics her.

'This is too, too much, you know. It's my only free period this century and I'm running around doing the Deputy Head's job for him, and the Head's job for her, and the Queen's job as well and I don't have another free until the year two thousand and fifty!'

They all laugh. Some older pupils pass by and jostle them. Gary's bag is knocked off his shoulder.

Gary   Hey, watch it!

He picks up his bag. The pupil mouths something at him.

Cor, did you hear that?

Karen   Leave it, Gary, they're a lot bigger than you.

Rina   That's my house, third one down on the left.

Gary   Bit big, isn't it?

Rina   Not really.

Gary   It's mega.

Rina   No, it isn't. Would you still be friends with me if I lived somewhere less posh, Gary?

Gary   Course I would.

Rina   Good, because you shouldn't judge people by where they live. 'Bye everybody.

Debbie	'Bye, Rina.
Karen	See you here tomorrow. Five to, OK?
Rina	Yes. 'Bye, Gary, and thanks.

Gary speaks in a posh voice.

Gary	Not at all, dear girl. Anything else I can do for you?
Rina	No, that will be all.

Rina walks towards her house. The others walk on.

Scene Eleven

Characters: Gary, Mrs Greene, Gary's Nan.

Gary's house. He has just arrived home. His mother is in the kitchen washing up.

Mrs Greene	Is that you, son?
Gary	No, it's the little green Martian.
Mrs Greene	Less of that lip. Where have you been all this time?
Gary	School, where else? You are daft sometimes.
Mrs Greene	Don't get so lippy or I'll give you such a clout. Why haven't you taken off those filthy shoes? I've cleaned all through today. If I see one scrap of mud anywhere –
Gary	I'm going to do my homework. Anything to eat?
Mrs Greene	No, I'm not having you under my feet now. Besides, I've just cleaned the floor. I don't want crumbs everywhere. You'll have to wait.
Gary	Oh, come on, Mum, I'm starving.
Mrs Greene	Don't you start, Gary. Go and see your Nan!

As he goes he quickly snatches an apple and a bag

of crisps. He disappears into the lounge where his Nan is sitting in an armchair knitting and watching television.

Gary's Nan   Hello, my boy. How are you?

Gary   Great, Nan, just great.

Gary's Nan   Good. I heard your Mum shouting. She been on at you again? Don't take no notice.

He sits on the sofa, opens up his crisps and offers her one.

No thanks, love, I haven't got my teeth in. Tell me all about your new school.

Scene Twelve

Characters: Debbie, Mr Carrington

Debbie's house later on. Her father arrives home. He is in his police uniform.

Mr C.   Hello, Princess. Sorry I'm late. We had a big shout on just as I was about to leave. Let's have a look at that new uniform. You look smashing. It suits you. So, how's my little girl been on her first day at big school?

Debbie   Dad, I'm not little any more.

Mr C.   Don't grow up too soon, love. I see too much of that in my job. You stay my little Princess for a while.

Debbie   Dad!

Mr C.   How did you get on?

Debbie   All right. Our new form teacher's quite nice and I have to sit next to a girl called Emma, and Karen sits next to Rina. We made friends with her but a boy in our class said a lot of horrible things to her at break, about being from Pakistan and things, but she isn't anyway.

Mr C.   I hope they put a stop to that.

Debbie   Yes, he had to see the teachers and he's got to stay behind all week, and he had to say he was sorry.

Mr C.   Good. So how do you like your new school then?

Debbie   It's all right.

Mr C.   Oh, as good as that, was it?

Debbie   I've got to go upstairs to get ready for tomorrow.

Mr C.   Duty calls and all that.

Debbie   Yes, Dad.

Mr C.   Tomorrow is another day.

Debbie   Yes, Dad.

Mr C.   The first day is always the worst.

Debbie   Yes, Dad.

Mr C.   Yes, Dad!

The End

SCHOOL PLAY

Jane Liddiard

List of Characters

Pupils
Karen
Debbie
Gary
Rina
Daniel
Gordon
Jatinder
Peter
Lisa
Russell
Carlton (Carl)
Amina
Kurio 1
Chorus 1, 2, 3
Narrators 1, 2, 3 ⎫
Football Fans ⎬ non-speaking
Several other Chorus members ⎭

Teachers
Ms Strange, English and Drama
Miss Solomons (Miss Sol.), Head of Music
Mrs Davies, Head of English
Mr Baxter, English
Mr Williams, P.T.

Parents
Rina's Mum
Mrs De Souza (Mrs De S. – Peter's Mum)

SCHOOL PLAY

Scene One

Characters: Debbie, Gary, Karen, Rina, Ms Strange, Miss Solomons, Mr Baxter.

The School Hall at lunchtime. A large number of pupils are milling around waiting for the teachers.

Debbie It's ever so noisy in here.

Karen Are you going to audition, Gary?

Gary Yeah, I fancy doing the pop star part – you know, with my guitar and that.

Debbie You won't get that part. You're not tall enough.

Gary Well, I'm growing. I'll be much taller by the start of the play.

Debbie Anyway, you're not handsome enough.

Gary You're not so pretty yourself, pig-face.

Ms Strange arrives with Miss Solomons and Mr Baxter. She trips over someone's bag and everyone laughs. They go on to the stage in the School Hall.

Ms Strange I hope your entrances will be less clumsy than mine. OK, listen carefully. We won't be doing any actual auditioning today because some of you need to look at the script. We'll do the auditioning on Thursday.

Mr Baxter For those of you who don't know, we are doing a play, a musical in fact, called *Ivory Man* by Ann Lovelace and Angela Allson.

Gary Sir, do you have to be good looking to be the pop star?

Mr Baxter Ah, well, I ... ah ... Perhaps Ms Strange would like

	to answer that question.
Ms Strange	Not necessarily, Gary, but you do have to be older and fairly tall. I'll probably be casting someone from the Upper School for this part.
Gary	Thought this was supposed to be a Lower School play. I'm going.
Ms Strange	No, don't go just yet, Gary. Miss Solomons is doing the music and she may have something for you.
Miss Sol.	I shall be needing quite a few musicians for this play, and not just orchestra players. We'll need to use a synthesiser, electric guitars and possibly a steel band.
Karen	What are you going in for, Debbie?
Debbie	Don't really know yet but I want to act. I did lots of plays at my other school and I go to drama lessons on Friday evenings.
Gary	Expect they'll give you all the parts then!
Debbie	Don't be horrible, Gary.
Rina	He doesn't mean it, Debbie, he's just feeling a bit stressed.
Karen	I don't want to act but I'd like to do some music, wouldn't you, Rina?
Rina	Yes, it sounds fun.
Gary	Ssh. Miss is talking.
Debbie	Ooh, get you! Since when have you ever wanted to listen to the teachers?
Gary	There! I didn't get none of that.

Gary shouts out.

What was that again, Miss?

| **Ms Strange** | I said, Gary, those of you interested in acting go to the Drama Studio now. Mr Baxter will take your names and give you a copy of the play as he will be helping me to produce and direct *Ivory Man*. |

Murmurs of 'Oooh!' The actors start to drift away.

Gary   Do you think she's going out with him?

Rina   Don't be daft. Why should she be going out with him?

Gary   Well, you know. I saw them talking together in the car park yesterday.

Karen   How naughty! Fancy two teachers talking to each other in the car park!

Gary digs Karen in the ribs.

Gary   Shut up, stupid.

Karen digs him back.

Karen   I'm not the one who's stupid. You are.

Debbie   See you later. I'm going to get a copy of the play.

Debbie goes along with all the other actors. Only the musicians are left.

Miss Sol. Listen please, everybody. (*Pause*) Right, this musical is set in a space station on Kuriosmos, which is a planet in outer space.

Gary   Never heard of it.

Miss Sol. Now, there is wide scope to use virtually every kind of musical instrument for this production. All I'm going to do today is to ask you to write down your names and the instruments you play on these pieces of paper. It's nice to see so many of you interested in the music for this production and I'm sure it's going to be a marvellous experience for everybody.

Gary   (*leaving*) Oh, yeah? Not even allowed to go in for what you want to.

Miss Sol. Gary, don't you want to act or do the music?

Gary   No, Miss Strange said I'm too small for the pop star and it's the only part I wanted.

Miss Sol. Don't give up too soon. I may need someone to play the guitar if the pop star can't.

Gary doesn't answer.

Give it a try.

Rina   Go on, Gary.

Gary   Nah, don't think so.

He goes off in a huff.

Scene Two

Characters: Rina, Debbie, Karen, Gary.

In the corridor the same day, on the way to lessons.

Rina   Gary wouldn't even put his name down for the music. I think he was a bit upset about being too small for the pop star part. He had his heart set on it.

Debbie   Bit daft, though. How could he think he was big enough for that part?

Rina   It is supposed to be a Lower School production.

Debbie   Yes, but he is rather short even for Lower School.

Rina   You'll get a part though, won't you, Debbie? You've done a lot of acting.

Debbie   Yes, but Miss said she'd be very fair and we'd all have to audition.

Rina   Bet you get a part. What do you fancy?

Debbie   Don't know, really. A Narrator or a Kurio. That's someone from outer space, from a planet called Kuriosmos. You have to sit in sort of space craft things on wheels all through the play.

Rina   Ugh! Worse than being in a school orchestra concert.

Debbie   No, I think it'll be great. We'll be all made up with silver make-up so we don't look like humans, and wearing amazing costumes and all that.

Gary catches up with them and taps Rina on the shoulder.

Gary   Cool!

Rina   Are you really not going to bother going in for the play?

Gary   Nah, what's the point? All the teachers' pets like Debbie will get the best parts, and who wants to strum a guitar off stage for some geezer who can't even play? Don't want to be in the stupid school play anyway. They can keep it and stuff it up their –

Rina   Gary!

Gary   – jumpers. I'd rather play football with my mates. Cheers.

He makes an imaginary kick at goal and then cheers and raises his hands as though he has scored, then he runs off. Rina shouts after him but Karen stops her.

Rina   Gary!

Karen   Leave him, Rina.

They go into the Art Room and collect their papers and other materials, which they put on a table. Gary hasn't got there yet.

Rina   He's really upset. Do you think we ought to tell Ms Strange about it?

Karen   Why?

Rina   I think he might go and do something stupid.

Debbie   That'll make a change.

Rina   No, seriously. You remember how he was when Mr Williams dropped him from the football team that time? He let all the footballs down just before the match.

Debbie   (*laughing*) Yes, and Mr Williams drove to his house and brought him back to school and made him blow them all up again. Then he had to walk all the way home.

Karen Do you really think he might go and do something stupid to the school play?

Rina I don't know, but I wouldn't put it past him. He gets a bit carried away sometimes.

Karen Yes, I know what you mean. Perhaps we ought to tell Miss after all.

Debbie But we might get him into trouble. I don't think we should tell.

Karen It's for his own good really, Debbie.

Rina Miss won't do anything. She's all right.

Debbie You tell her! I'm not going to. Gary's OK.

Karen We're not saying he isn't.

Debbie No, but you're going to grass him up.

Debbie gets up and goes to another table to sit with someone else.

Debbie You're not my friends any more!

Scene Three

Characters: Ms Strange, Miss Solomons.

The Staffroom at about 5.30 pm. It is empty.
Ms Strange enters and collapses into a chair.

Ms Strange What a day! It's days like these that make me feel that I never want to teach again.

Miss Solomons enters and goes to the kitchen area.

Miss Sol. Coffee, Catherine?

Ms Strange Oh, yes, please.

Miss Sol. I think we've got a slight problem on our hands. Gary Greene.

Ms Strange Yes, I know. I do feel sorry for him but it can't be helped. I've given the part he wants to Carlton King and Lisa Romero has the other. I could just imagine her reaction if she was playing opposite Gary. It would be like a giraffe with a rabbit!

Miss Sol. I agree, but I shall still try to persuade him to be involved with the music.

Ms Strange Well, if that fails I may try to rope him in backstage.

Miss Sol. You're brave. Do you think the scenery will survive!

Ms Strange I haven't got much choice really, and anyway, doesn't fortune favour the brave?

Miss Sol. Not if we're talking about Gary Greene.

Miss Solomons shrugs her shoulders and hands over the coffee. Ms Strange raises her eyebrows, smiles and sighs.

Scene Four

Characters: Mr Williams, Gary, Daniel.

Some days later in the Gym. Gary is hanging by his hands from the swing bar absolutely still. Suddenly, the door bursts open and 7S boys race in followed by Mr Williams. They form two lines at opposite sides of the Gym and stand with their hands by their sides.

Daniel   Sir, Sir, look at Gary, Sir!

Mr Williams walks smartly over to Gary.

Mr Williams   Greene, what the hell are you doing, boy?

Gary   Aagh! Aagh!

Daniel   He's gone all green, Sir!

Mr Williams   Quiet.

Gary   Oohh!

Mr Williams   Ah, we want to get down now, do we? Uncomfortable up there, are we?

Daniel   Sir. Do you think he's training for the Olympics, Sir?

Mr Williams   If you don't shut it, Smith, *you'll* be training for the Olympics.

Gary   Sir, my arms have gone all numb.

Mr Williams   Like your brains then are they, boy?

Gary   Please, Sir, I can't move. I've got pins and needles in my feet. Aagh!

Mr Williams   This is not a sewing class, Greene. This is PT.

Daniel   Yeah, Physical Training for Pathetic Twits.

Mr Williams   Right, Smith. Start running on the spot and don't stop till I tell you.

He groans but does so. Gary lets go. Mr Williams catches him and lowers him on to the floor, moaning. Gary rubs his arms and legs, writhing about. The others are laughing.

Mr Williams Quiet, you lot!

There is instant silence. Mr Williams helps Gary to get up. He hops about painfully.

Mr Williams Better now, boy?

Gary Yes, Sir.

Daniel He's like a constipated duck.

Mr Williams Right, Smith, I've had enough of you. See me at the end of the day and don't be late.

Daniel (*moaning*) Yes, Sir.

Mr Williams Greene, you know you're not allowed in this gym on your own, and definitely not on equipment like this without someone standing by to help you. Well?

Gary I was trying to stretch, Sir.

Mr Williams Stretch? What do you mean, *stretch*?

Gary I wanted to get a bit taller, Sir.

Mr Williams If you want to grow I suggest you ask your mother to give you some Baby Bio in your cocoa, or stick you in a Growmore bag.

The others are laughing.

Shut up, you lot, or I'll make you hang from the bars for half an hour. Right, let's get on. We've wasted enough time already this morning. OK, everyone to the other end of the Gym.

The boys immediately run to the end of the Gym, Gary hobbling off after them. Daniel is still running on the spot desperately out of breath.

Mr Williams Come on, look sharp! Start running to the other end and back again and don't stop till I tell you. Come on, Smith, get in there and look lively.

Daniel Oh no, not more running!

Scene Five

Characters: Mr Williams, Ms Strange.

The Staffroom later that day. Ms Strange is sitting at a table marking. Mr Williams comes in and looks around.

Mr Williams Ah, Catherine, I've been looking for you. Can I have a word? It's Gary Greene. The kid's off his head. I found him hanging from the swing bar in the Gym this morning. Seems he's trying to stretch himself to be taller.

Ms Strange Oh, I know what this is all about. He wanted a part in the school play but he's too small.

Mr Williams What's a kid like him doing wanting to be in the school play? What he needs is some real discipline and to get his head down and learn something for a change.

Ms Strange puts her pen down angrily.

Ms Strange Are you saying that only the good pupils should be allowed to be in the school play, Mervyn?

Mr Williams Well, it's always the same, isn't it? These bad lads get a part in the play and start strutting around the school telling us they've got to have time off our lessons for rehearsals. Telling us, mind. Not asking.

Ms Strange stands up and gathers her books.

Ms Strange Hasn't it ever occurred to you that all these 'bad lads' want is to be good at something? Just one little thing in their lives. If it's sport or science, it's OK. But a bit of drama or music and that's definitely out!

She flounces off angrily. Mr Williams looks bewildered.

Scene Six

Characters: Karen, Debbie, Rina, Gary, Daniel.

The school next day. Debbie, Rina and Karen stop by the noticeboard.

Rina   Karen and me are both doing the music for *Ivory Man*.

Debbie   Great.

Karen   The cast list is up, Debbie.

Debbie   Oh no, I don't want to look! Have a look for me, will you?

Karen and Rina look at the list.

Karen   Wow, Debbie, you're one of the Narrators! That's a great part. Well done.

Debbie   Thanks. Who's the male pop star?

Karen   Carlton King. He's in Year Ten.

Debbie   Ooh, I like him. He's lovely. Who's got the other part?

Karen   Lisa Romero.

Debbie   Oh, not her. She's horrible. She can't even act and I bet she's after Carlton.

They go into their classroom and sit on the tables.

Rina   Have you ever forgotten your lines?

Debbie   Loads of times. Usually people help you out by talking a load of rubbish until you remember them again, but once I forgot a whole load and I couldn't carry on. I was in this play and there was only me and Gerard O'Hare on stage. Do you remember him, Karen?

Karen   Yes, he had ginger hair and was brilliant at maths.

Debbie   Anyway, we had a massive amount to say but half-way through I dried – that's when you can't remember anything. The Prompt gave me my line twice but I couldn't remember the rest so I just walked – well, ran – into the wings and Gerard was left there all on his own.

Rina What happened?

Debbie He stayed there for a minute or two then he turned to the audience and said, '*I think she needs to go to the toilet.*' And I did!

Gary and Daniel arrive. Gary is holding something behind his back. Daniel sits next to Debbie, who instantly moves away from him.

Gary Well, go on then.

Debbie Go on what?

Daniel Congratulate him.

Debbie What for?

Gary hands her the Cast List.

Gary Look at this. Down there.

Rina Gary, you're doing backstage!

Gary Yeah, that's me. Leader of the gang. Very important.

Debbie Who said so?

Daniel Miss did. So there.

Debbie You should put that list back. Someone else might want to see it.

Gary mimics her by mouthing words but doesn't actually say anything. She makes a face at him.

Karen Have you got a part, Daniel?

Daniel No, not interested. Prefer my football.

Gary You're jealous because you've only got an acting part.

Debbie *Only?* Acting's the most important thing.

Daniel Not as important as him. Miss gave it to him special.

Debbie	Don't be daft. Who are the audience going to see on the night, you or me?
Gary	You – unfortunately for them. They'll all go home feeling sick.
Daniel	Running away in fright, more like.
Debbie	I'll get you two for that.
Daniel	Have to catch us first!

They run off laughing.

Scene Seven

Characters: Ms Strange, Gary, Kurio 1, Chorus 1, 2, 3, Gordon, Jatinder, Carlton.

The School Hall some weeks later. Rehearsals for the play are well under way. Ms Strange is sitting at a table in front of the stage. Kurio 1 is on stage.

Ms Strange Right, we'll go from the end of Scene Two. Quiet everyone. Cue sound.

There is the sound of a noisy football crowd from a cassette player.

Kurio 1 shouts over the noise.

Kurio 1 *Notice how the …*

Ms Strange No, you're supposed to turn the sound down *before* you speak. Again, please.

The sound of the football crowd is played again. Kurio 1 waits a few moments and then he mimes pressing a remote control unit. Some seconds later the noise fades down.

Ms Strange	Try to cut the sound on cue. Keep going.
Kurio 1	*Notice how the leader of the gods is about to give his blessing.*
Ms Strange	OK, here is where we shall have some live music to accompany the football fans singing their song but as we haven't got that yet …

Gary pokes his head round the curtains onto the stage.

Gary	When's that going to be, Miss?
Ms Strange	(*sighing*) Probably next week. Now remember, Gary, you're not supposed to keep coming on to the stage and interrupting the acting.
Gary	Oops, sorry, Miss.

He disappears. There is a loud crash offstage accompanied by shouts of 'Gary!' *He reappears.*

Gary	Sorry, Miss, I fell over some scenery.
Ms Strange	Give me strength.

She waits then shouts

Football Fans, you should be on!

Chorus 1 comes on stage.

Chorus 1	Didn't hear our cue, Miss.

The crowd of Football Fans comes noisily on stage. They form two lines waving their scarves. Then they all stop.

Ms Strange	Don't stand there looking gormless. Start singing your song now.
Chorus 1	Oh, yeah.

Ms Strange gets up and goes to the foot of the stage.

Ms Strange	You're meant to be idolising football fans, not a bunch of daffodils. Show some enthusiasm! Everybody off stage and come on again.

They moan and troop off stage. Ms Strange holds her head in her hands in frustration and sits down again wearily. They come on again, then there is silence.

Carlton   What's the matter now? I want to get home. There's a good film on.

Ms Strange   Who's next?

Carlton   That weedy little kid, what's his name?

Chorus 2   Peter De Souza.

Chorus 1   He's not here, Miss.

Chorus 3   He's got to go out with his Mum tonight, so she said he had to be home early.

Ms Strange   How am I supposed to hold rehearsals if people pick and choose when they want to attend? Tell him I want to see him tomorrow. Right, let's move on.

Carlton   I knew he was a dead loss.

Gary   I could sing that bit for you, Miss. I know it.

Carlton   Not another Year Seven prat! This is all we need.

Ms Strange   OK, Gary.

Gary comes on stage. She waits. Nothing happens. Carlton pushes him.

Carlton   Get on with it, Greene.

Gary   (*singing*) *When baby's rattle –*

Gordon shouts from the wings.

Gordon   Baby, baby Gary!

Gary   Aw, Miss.

Ms Strange   Who was that?

Gordon   Dunno, Miss.

Ms Strange   (*exasperated*) Never mind. Carry on, Gary.

Gary   I'm not singing it if someone's going to take the mickey.

Carlton   Nobody's taking the mickey. It was just a joke. Get on with it, Greene.

Gary   *When baby's rattle I would shake,*
             Sitting in my pram –

Gordon   He's still in it. Give him a dummy!

Gary   Right, that's it. I'm not doing this any more.

He storms off.

Ms Strange is really angry and marches up to the foot of the stage again.

Ms Strange   Who was that?

Gordon grins stupidly.

Gordon   Me, Miss.

Ms Strange   OK, Gordon, that's your lot for the day and possibly the rest of the play.

Gordon   I was only joking.

Ms Strange   Being a member of the backstage crew is no joke. You can go. Now.

He goes. Everyone cheers.

Kurio 1   Nice one, Miss.

Ms Strange   Let's get on. Gary.

Gary   *When baby's rattle I would shake,*
             Sitting in my pram,
             I was just in training for
             Being a football fan.

Gary stops singing and grins at everybody.

Gary   Was that all right, Miss?

Ms Strange   (*sighing*) Wonderful, Gary. Chorus 2.

Gary   Did you hear that? Miss said I was marvellous. I only did a little bit. Good, wasn't it?

Jatinder speaks from the wings.

Jatinder Shut up, Greene.

Ms Strange   Exit noisily everybody after marching round the stage once. Whistles blowing, lots of cheering and shouting. End of scene and I think end of rehearsal. Jatinder, I'd like to see you. The rest can go.

They go talking and jostling. Jatinder comes off stage and goes over to Ms Strange.

Ms Strange Jatinder, you're Stage Manager. That means you're in complete control backstage, so I'd appreciate it if you could keep everyone else under control too.

Jatinder I try to, Miss, but they won't shut up.

Ms Strange Report them to me and I'll have a word with them. And Gary must be made to realise that he can't keep popping up on stage whilst the actors are on.

Jatinder He's impossible. He never keeps still. Wouldn't it be better to get rid of him?

Ms Strange No, but we have to try to curb his natural exuberance.

Jatinder I'll do my best.

Ms Strange Yes, I know you will. At least you're one person I can rely on. Don't take this too personally. You're doing very well.

Scene Eight

Characters: Rina, Rina's Mum, Amina (Rina's sister)

Rina arrives home from school. Her mother is watching TV. Rina goes into the lounge and takes off her coat.

Rina Where's Dad?

Rina's Mum He's gone to New York on business. You said goodbye to him this morning. You've got a memory

	like a sieve. How did your day go?
Rina	It was all right. We had a supply teacher in for French because Mrs O'Donnell was away. The boys thought they could play him up but he soon had them under control, except that he didn't know any of our names. Every time he asked someone their name the boys would give somebody else's name, and it all got a bit stupid.
Rina's Mum	Don't these people ever want to learn anything?
Rina	No, a lot of them don't. Especially French. Where's Amina?
Rina's Mum	Upstairs in her room working. How's the music for the play going?
Rina	We're nearly ready to join in with the main part of the play. It's great. Miss Solomons is quite funny sometimes. Debbie's got an acting part. She's done a lot before.
Rina's Mum	Oh, by the way, I had a letter from Dipak.
Rina	(*excitedly*) You might have told me! Where is it? Let me see it, please.
Rina's Mum	I've got it here, don't panic. I'll go and get the supper while you read it.

She hands Rina the letter and goes out. Rina grabs it eagerly and opens it. She reads and sighs occasionally or tuts. Then she shouts out loud.

Rina	Oh, no, Mum, they can't! They can't do this!

Her mother returns.

Rina's Mum	Whatever is it, child?
Rina	They're going to move Dipak. Mum, they can't. It's too far away.
Rina's Mum	Calm down, calm down. Shouting isn't going to get you anywhere. Now let's sit down quietly and talk about this.

Rina pushes her away.

Rina	No, I don't want to talk.
Rina's Mum	We have to, darling. You can't change things by shouting about them.

Rina's sister comes into the room.

Amina	What's all the fuss?
Rina	Nothing.
Amina	Then what's all the shouting about?
Rina	Nothing. Mind your own business.
Amina	Mum?
Rina's Mum	She's just heard about Dipak.
Amina	I know how you feel, Rina, but it's for the best. There's a better regime there and he'll be able to continue his studies, which he can't do at his present place.
Rina	But we won't be able to see him as often.
Amina	No, but sometimes we have to do what's best for others and not ourselves.
Rina	Oh, so you think I'm selfish wanting to see my own brother.
Rina's Mum	We don't think that. It will be better for Dipak at this other place even though it's much farther away, and we must put his welfare first.
Rina	They could have put him in a better place nearer, I know they could. It's only because he's Asian that they're doing this.
Rina's Mum	Rina, I don't want to hear you talking like that.
Rina	Why not? It's true, isn't it?
Rina's Mum	That's what got him into trouble in the first place. We shouldn't be creating a fuss.
Rina	That's right. Just lie low and don't say anything. That's what parents always say.
Amina	That's not true, Rina, Mum gets it too. People in the street can be just as bad.
Rina	I hate you! All of you! You don't care about Dipak!

She runs out of the room up to her bedroom. Amina tries to stop her but she is too quick.

Amina You carry on with the supper, Mum. I'll go up and talk to her.

Amina goes to Rina's bedroom. She is lying on her bed with her head buried in the pillow.

Amina Rina? ... Come on.

She goes over to the bed, sits on the edge and puts her arm round Rina's shoulders.

I know how you feel. We're all upset about it.

Rina Everybody knew except me! Why do you always treat me like a baby? They let you do everything.

Amina Mum and Dad worry about you. There's a lot of nasty people about these days. All they see are awful stories in the papers. (*Pause*) And there's what happened to Dipak.

Rina It wasn't his fault!

Amina But it happened, Rina, and we've got to accept it.

Rina Why don't you believe him?

Amina I do but no one else does – least of all the police and the courts.

Rina But he didn't do it. He was there with the others but he didn't do anything wrong.

Amina You can be guilty in the eyes of the law even if you are there and don't actually do anything. Another boy got knifed, Rina, and he's fighting for his life.

Rina He was a racist. If Dipak's friend had done nothing they would have got hurt instead of him. Why don't they see that?

Amina I don't know, but there's nothing we can do about it, Rina, and upsetting yourself like this isn't doing you any good, and it's not helping Mum either.

Rina You're just like everybody else. You don't care! You don't care!

She starts to cry again. Amina tries to comfort her. At first Rina pushes her away, then she lets her sister hug her.

Amina Mum and Dad are doing everything they can to have the case re-opened but it takes a long time just to get anybody to listen. Have you told any of your friends about it?

Rina No, and you're not to tell them either!

Amina OK, OK, I won't tell them if you really don't want me to but it does help, you know.

Rina No!

Amina Well, what about a teacher then?

Rina No!

Amina Rina, listen to me. You've got to talk to somebody about this. It's making you really unhappy and your work is beginning to suffer.

Rina No! No! No!

Amina What about Ms Strange? She's really nice and she would understand.

Rina I can't.

Amina Why not?

Rina She'd tell all the other teachers.

Amina She wouldn't tell them all. She might tell some, like Mrs Davies, but *she* knows anyway. I've already talked to her about it. Look, it might help in some way. It would help them to understand why your work is suffering and it would be good to talk to someone who's outside the family ... Please, Rina, I really think you need to talk to someone.

Rina OK, but will you talk to Ms Strange for me first?

Amina Of course I will. Now, are you going to come and have some supper and show Mum you're feeling better? She's quite upset too, you know.

Rina Yes.

Amina Good, because I'm starving!

Scene Nine

Characters: Debbie, Karen, Rina, Lisa.

It is after a play rehearsal. Everybody is milling around.

Rina   I'm exhausted! I never knew there'd be so much waiting around and doing nothing.

Debbie   It's always like this at rehearsals but on the night it all goes so fast.

Rina   Really?

Debbie   Yes, I'm not joking. Once I had ever such a long scene with masses to say, and on the first night of the performance I came offstage and thought I'd missed half of it.

Rina   You have to keep stopping so much, it's very annoying.

Karen   And all those people backstage to do props, and lighting, and costumes ...

Rina   ... and prompt and sound ...

Debbie   ... and directing and producing.

They all laugh. Lisa comes over and stands by them aggressively.

Lisa   What's all this racket about?

Lisa notices Debbie.

Isn't it time you were tucked up in bed?

Karen   Mind your own business, Lisa. She's not doing anything to you.

Lisa   Oh, yeah, and who asked you to speak? She knows what this is all about, don't you, dear little Debbie?

Karen   You leave her alone or ...

Lisa   Yeah?

Karen   Just leave her alone.

Lisa   I'll do what I like, so don't you threaten *me*.

Rina   She wasn't threatening you.

Lisa   Oh, you're at it now, are you? You've got a sister in the sixth form, haven't you?

Rina   Yes, so what?

Lisa   So don't think that's going to protect you.

She speaks to Debbie, poking her on the shoulder.

Lisa   Keep away. Know what I mean?

Debbie   I haven't done anything wrong.

Lisa   Not yet you haven't but I'm watching you – and it would be such a shame to spoil that pretty little face of yours, wouldn't it?

She glares at Debbie to let the message sink in, and then walks off arrogantly. Debbie is shaking.

Rina   What was that all about?

Debbie   She thinks I want to take Carlton away from her.

Rina   She must be mad. Sorry, Debbie, I don't mean any offence but well, you know.

Debbie   Yes, I know. I don't stand a chance but I like him. He's ever so nice and I don't see why I shouldn't talk to him if he talks to me. He doesn't mind me talking to him.

Karen   Yes, but Lisa does and she's a lot bigger than you, so be careful.

Debbie   Do you really think she'd do anything?

Karen   I wouldn't put it past her.

Debbie   Oh!

Rina   Never mind, she probably won't. Come on, it's getting late. We'd better go home.

Scene Ten

Characters: Ms Strange, Miss Solomons, Carlton, Lisa, Gary, Peter, Mrs De Souza.

It is the end of a full play rehearsal.

Ms Strange That's it, everybody, thank you, except for Carlton and Lisa. I'd like to run through your bit again very quickly. What's going on?

Mrs De Souza has marched noisily into the Hall waving her arms about in agitation.

Mrs De S. Who's in charge here? Take me to what's-her-name – that woman who's the form teacher. The one with the funny name. I've had enough of this.

Ms Strange Do you wish to see me?

Mrs De S. What time do you call this? I was expecting my son to be involved in a rehearsal, not an attempt to get into the Guinness Book of Records!

Ms Strange I admit it has been a little longer than we had hoped this evening.

Mrs De S. *A little*? I've been waiting in my car for over half an hour! These children do have suppers to eat and homework to do and homes to go to – even if you teachers don't.

Ms Strange Yes, indeed, Mrs De Souza, I do apologise. Peter, would you come, please. Your mother's here waiting for you.

Peter appears rather sheepishly.

Mrs De S. Ah, there you are. Do you know what time it is?

Peter Yes, Mother.

Mrs De S. I don't expect to be kept waiting for over half an hour.

Peter	No, Mother.
Mrs De S.	Are you ready to go? Look at you. Have you been rolling in the mud?
Peter	I don't know, Mother.
Mrs De S.	What am I going to do with you? Put your tie straight and do those buttons up and don't forget your school bag. I hope that's not covered in mud too. Have you got the right homework books? Do I have to do everything for you?

She ushers him out. Gary marches about like Mrs De Souza, mimicking her.

Gary	Do I have to do everything for you? Yes, Mother. Come along, Peter, put your nappy on. Yes, Mother. And stick your dummy in your mouth. Yes, Mother, no, Mother, three bags full, Mother.
Miss Sol.	All I want to do now is go over the singing. So just Carlton and Lisa for this, please.

Gary lurks in the wings unseen. Carl and Lisa stand upstage and listen to instructions from Miss Solomons.

Miss Sol.	You have a music cue and a movement cue, so watch from the wings and run on with lots of enthusiasm to the apron stage where the microphones are. Right, if Sound's ready we'll go. Music. Audio screams. And on.

Carlton and Lisa run on to the stage from opposite sides and rush towards the apron stage. However, Carlton slips and cannot stop himself from falling. He yells as he crashes on to the floor. Everyone looks horrified and the teachers rush forward as the music stops erratically. Carlton is writhing about on the floor in agony and Lisa is screaming.

Lisa	Carl, Carl, what's happened?
Carlton	Aagh, aagh! Oh, my leg, aagh!
Ms Strange	Oh, my goodness. OK, Carlton, try to keep still.

Carlton	Aaagh! My leg! My leg!
Ms Strange	Stay still. Don't move. You'll only make it worse.
Lisa	Oh, Miss, is he going to be all right?
Ms Strange	Yes, Lisa, I think he may have broken his leg but he'll live.
Lisa	Oh, Carl.
Carlton	It hurts. It really hurts, Miss.
Ms Strange	I expect it does, but try to keep still or you may do some more damage. Ruth, you'd better call for an ambulance. It could be broken. And see if there's anyone around who can give us a hand. We need a First Aid box.
Gary	Shall I find the Caretaker, Miss?

Miss Solomons is surprised to see him.

Miss S.	Ah ... yes, Gary, that's a good idea.

He races off. Lisa is crying.

Lisa	Oh, Miss, is he going to be all right?
Ms Strange	Yes, Lisa, of course he is, but you won't help by having hysterics. He's in a lot of pain so help me to keep him still.
Lisa	Oh, Carl, does it hurt?
Carlton	Of course it hurts!
Lisa	Oh, you poor thing.
Carlton	I'll be all right, don't fuss. Oh, man!
Lisa	He's gone all pale, Miss. What's the matter, what's the matter?
Ms Strange	Lisa, keep calm. He's in shock, that's all.

She speaks to herself.

Oh, no. Can anything else go wrong?

Scene Eleven

Characters: Ms Strange, Miss Solomons, Mrs Davies, Gary.

The English Office the next day. Ms Strange and Mrs Davies are talking.

Mrs Davies So what's the damage to Carlton, Catherine?

Ms Strange He's broken his leg. He'll be in hospital for a few days and then he'll have to rest for a week. There's no question of his resuming his part in the play. I don't know what to do. We go into the Technical and Dress rehearsals tomorrow and then we're into four nights of performance and I'm without one of my leads. It's a nightmare! It's been one thing after another with this play.

Mrs Davies There must be another Year Ten who's capable of this part, surely?

Miss Sol. It's not so much being capable as being a quick learner. Carlton had solos, choruses, and special choreography. You don't learn all that in five minutes.

There is a knock at the door. Gary pops his head round and grins at them.

Gary Can I see you a minute, Miss?

Ms Strange Not now, Gary.

Gary It's really important, Miss. It's about the play.

Ms Strange Later, Gary!

Gary Oh!

Gary goes away looking very disappointed.

Mrs Davies I think you should go and see him, Catherine. He has come specially.

She goes out and sees Gary standing outside in the corridor. She calls him.

Ms Strange Yes, Gary, what can I do for you? – bearing in mind that I have a full day's teaching and a school play crashing down around my ears.

Gary That's where I can help you, Miss. I can do Carlton's part.

Ms Strange Gary …

Gary No, listen a minute, yeah. I know I'm not as big as him, right, but I can sing just as well and I know all the moves, yeah, because I've seen it done loads of times.

Ms Strange Look, Gary, I know you're trying to be helpful but I really don't think it's going to work. Thanks all the same.

Gary is desperately upset.

Gary OK, Miss, but I know I can do it. I know I can!

He runs off.

Ms Strange Gary, Gary! Oh no, I didn't handle that very well.

She goes back into the English Office as Miss Solomons appears and follows her in.

Miss Sol. More problems?

Ms Strange In a way. Gary Greene thinks he can do Carlton's part and of course I had to turn him down. He was terribly disappointed and ran off before I had a chance to explain.

Miss Sol. He probably could, you know.

Ms Strange What?

Miss Sol. Yes, honestly. He's been singing the pop star's songs as part of his music assessment and he's seen all the moves, so I wouldn't turn him down if I were you.

Ms Strange What about Lisa?

Miss Sol. What about her? She's got to realise what desperate straits we're in. She'll just have to swap the prince for the frog and lump it.

Ms Strange What if she refuses to play alongside Gary?

Miss Sol. She'd better not or I'll blacklist her for every other musical. I'll see her about it myself. She's a bit mouthy but we get on well. She likes music.

Ms Strange Bless you, Ruth, what would I do without you?

Miss Sol. Run away to sea, perhaps?

They all laugh.

Miss Sol. There, that's cheered you up. I'll go and find Gary right away and give him the good news.

She goes out.

Mrs Davies Catherine, while we're on our own, a word about Rina Gupta. Her sister Amina came to see me. She asked my advice about you talking to Rina about some trouble at home.

Ms Strange Ah, that might explain a lot. What's it about?

Mrs Davies The family don't want it to be generally known so it has to be treated in the strictest confidence. Rina has an older brother, Dipak.

Ms Strange Oh? I thought there were only her and her sister.

Mrs Davies That's what most people think. The brother is away in Youth Custody. Apparently, he got involved in an incident where a young white boy was stabbed. The boy was part of a notorious racist gang who went around taunting Asians and sometimes attacking them. Dipak and his friends were set upon that night but one of them had decided to carry a knife. I understand that Dipak wasn't involved in the actual stabbing, and he didn't know that his friend was carrying a knife, but since he was there he was convicted all the same. That's the law, I'm afraid. Naturally, Rina's very upset about it and can't understand why her brother has been blamed for something he didn't actually do.

Ms Strange I can understand that and it explains a lot. She's
hanging around with Emily and Vikki's crowd.
Hardly her type, those two.

Mrs Davies Mm, it's a familiar pattern when something's wrong.
I presume her work's suffering as well?

Ms Strange Yes, it's gone down badly and she's one of the
brightest in my class. I've had several complaints
filtering through.

Mrs Davies We can't do much about her choice of friends but
we can do something about the work.

Ms Strange Right, I'll see her today if I can. Lunchtime probably
– I'm going to need every minute after school to
rehearse with Gary. Poor Rina, it's a lot to cope with
at her age.

Scene Twelve

Characters: Mr Baxter, Ms Strange, Karen, Debbie.

*It is the full Dress Rehearsal of the play and
residents of an old people's home have been invited
to watch. All is going well until Mr Baxter discovers
that Debbie is not in position waiting to go on for
her next scene.*

Mr Baxter Where is Debbie? What a time to go off. Prompt,
will you get ready to read in Debbie's part.

Ms Strange comes up to them.

Ms Strange What's the panic?

Mr Baxter Debbie Carrington's gone AWOL and we don't
know where she is.

Ms Strange	I'll go and look for her.

Ms Strange leaves the Hall and goes into the corridor. Karen is hurrying towards her.

Ms Strange   Oh, Karen, have you seen Debbie? She's meant to be on stage.

Karen   Yes, Miss, I was just coming to find you. She's in the Girls' toilets. She's all upset and says she can't go back on stage.

Ms Strange   What a time to get stage fright!

Karen   It's not stage fright, Miss. It's Lisa. She's threatening to beat Debbie up. She thinks Debbie's after Carlton so she keeps having a go at her.

They go to the Girls' toilets. Debbie is dabbing at her eyes with a tissue.

Ms Strange   Now, Debbie what's all this about? You're due on stage any moment.

Debbie   I can't go on, Miss.

Ms Strange   Nonsense! You're one of my most experienced and best actors. If it's Lisa you're worried about then don't be. I'll speak to her. But right now our Hall is full of old people all enjoying the performance and I don't want to let them down. Do you?

Debbie   No, Miss.

Ms Strange   Good. So dry your eyes and get out there and sock it to them. OK?

Debbie rushes off with Karen. Ms Strange lets out a huge sigh.

Scene Thirteen

Characters: Ms Strange, Lisa.

The Dress Rehearsal has finished. The curtains are closed and as the applause dies away great excitement breaks out. Ms Strange comes on stage.

Ms Strange   OK, everybody, take a break while the audience leaves the Hall, then I want a briefing before you go. Lisa, where are you?

Lisa   Here, Miss.

Ms Strange   Come with me, please. We'll have that talk now.

Lisa   Do I have to?

Ms Strange   Yes, you do.

Lisa   This is stupid. All over some little git of a Year Seven.

Ms Strange   I'll decide what's stupid, Lisa, if you don't mind. I understand you've been bullying Debbie Carrington.

Lisa   *Bullying?* Don't make me laugh.

Ms Strange   So what has been going on?

Lisa   I just told her to keep away from Carl, that's all.

Ms Strange   That's all? Lisa, are you chewing gum?

Lisa   What if I am?

Ms Strange   Not when you're talking to me you don't. Get rid of it immediately.

Lisa sticks her gum on the wall. Ms Strange stares very hard at her and she backs down and removes the chewing gum from the wall and scrunches it in her hand.

Lisa   Look, she was after my bloke, right? I just warned her off, that's all.

Ms Strange   Lisa, how old are you?

Lisa   Nearly sixteen.

Ms Strange	Nearly sixteen and you think that a twelve-year-old is a threat to your relationship with a boy in Year Ten?
Lisa	Well, she hasn't stopped going after him since the play started.
Ms Strange	Grow up, Lisa. She's a Year Seven. She's got a crush on him, that's all!
Lisa	I don't care. I want her to keep away from him. She's even been to the hospital to see him. It's none of her business. All I did was tell her to stay away.
Ms Strange	You threatened to beat her up. Not only is that categorically against the school rules but she was so frightened by it that she nearly didn't come back on stage this afternoon.
Lisa	It's not my fault.
Ms Strange	I think it is. Do you understand?
Lisa	She isn't getting Carl off me.
Ms Strange	All this isn't about Debbie, Lisa. It's about you. You are so unsure of yourself that you are terrified of losing Carl. Doesn't say much for your relationship, does it?
Lisa	Oh, that's nice, isn't it? Tell me off about my boyfriend. You've no right to say that.
Ms Strange	I have every right to ensure that you behave in a civilised manner and do not put this production at risk. Understood? … I'm speaking to you.
Lisa	Yeah, all right, there's no need to keep going on at me.

Ms Strange goes. Lisa sticks her tongue out, then slaps the gum back on the wall.

Scene Fourteen

Characters: Gary, Peter, Russell, Jatinder.

It is the Finale of the play on the last night and everyone not on stage is in a large classroom used as their waiting room. Some of the boys are playing football with a rolled-up sock. Others are playing on Game Boys, or watching television.

Gary   And it's Andy Cole taking a glorious pass from midfield. Round one defender, two, three. Shoot! Yeah, goal!

Jatinder   Shut up, Greene, they'll hear you in the audience.

Gary   What, with all that singing and music?

Jatinder   Yes, we're not that far away.

Russell   You ought to tell that lot to keep the telly down. They're making more noise than we are.

Jatinder   OK, but you keep your noise down, too.

He moves off.

Russell   He's bossy, isn't he?

Gary   Yeah, and he's in charge and he's bigger than you so it's no good complaining.

Russell   Come on, it's boring in here. Let's go outside.

Gary   Yeah, it's too hot in here anyway.

They leave. Jatinder comes back.

Jatinder   Where's Greene and Morris?

Peter   They've gone outside.

Jatinder   What?

Peter   Outside. They said they were too hot so they've gone out.

Jatinder   Oh, no, the idiots. They're not allowed outside and anyway we've got the curtain call soon.

Peter   Do you want me to go and look for them?

Jatinder   Could you?

Peter   Yes, no problem. I think I know where they'll be.

Scene Fifteen

Characters: Peter, Gary, Russell.

Peter moves to the front of the stage.

Peter   Gary, Russell, are you there? Jatinder wants you back.

Gary mimicks him from offstage.

Gary   Gary, Russell, are you there?

Peter   Where are you?

Gary   Over here.

Russell   Over there.

Peter   Where?

Gary   Here.

Russell   There.

Gary   And everywhere.

They laugh.

Peter   No, come on, stop messing about.

Gary   Little Bo Peep has lost his sheep.

Russell   And doesn't know where to find them.

Peter   It's nearly time for the curtain call.

Gary   Leave them alone …

Russell   … and they'll come home.

Peter   I'm going in if you're going to be daft.

Gary   Ready for roast and mint sauce!

Peter   If you want to be daft, that's your problem.

He starts to go.

Russell   Hold on, mate, don't get so shirty. We're just coming.

Peter   Where are you?

Russell   Up here.

Peter   Where?

Russell   On the roof. Where else? The moon?

Peter   What are you doing up there?

Russell   Looking at the stars.

Peter   What?

Russell   We are *hobserving* the Milky Way.

Peter   What?

Gary   The Galaxy.

Peter   What?

Russell   Eating some chocolate, you berk.

Peter   You're not supposed to do that. Miss didn't want anyone being sick.

Gary   Why do you think we're up here? I should move out the way if I were you.

Peter   Come on, the play's nearly ended.

Gary   Keep your hair on. We're coming down, so stay away from that drainpipe or I'll drop on your head!

Russell   Might do him some good.

Peter   You're not allowed on the roof.

Russell   So, who's going to tell?

Gary appears beside Peter. He looks up.

Gary   Come on, Russ.

Russell is heard from offstage.

Russell   I can't.

Gary   What?

Russell   I can't, I'm scared of heights.

Gary   But you got up there.

Russell   Yes, but I wasn't looking down then.

Gary   Aw, come on, don't be a lemonhead.

Russell   I can't, Gary, honest.

Gary   Now what are we going to do?

Russell   You'll have to get someone.

Gary   Not likely. We'll be in dead trouble. Half a mo, I know what.

Russell   What?

Gary   There's a ladder by the Caretaker's shed. We'll use that.

Russell   But he might hear you.

Gary   No, not a chance. He's deaf so he'll have the telly on full blast. Peter and me'll get it, won't we, Pete?

Peter sounds very unsure.

Peter   I don't know.

Gary   Yes, you will, mate.

Gary and Peter go off in search of the ladder.

Scene Sixteen

Characters: Jatinder, Debbie, Mr Baxter, Gary.

In the waiting room Jatinder is getting nervous and impatient.

Jatinder   Where have that lot got to? It's practically time for the curtain call. I'll kill that Greene and Morris when I catch up with them.

Debbie   Shall I go and look for them?

Jatinder   (*panicking*) No, stay where you are! I don't want anyone else missing.

Debbie   Should we tell Ms Strange?

Jatinder   Not just yet. She's got enough on her plate. I'll deal with this. If necessary we'll do the Finale without them. Oh, just wait till I catch up with Greene. I know he's behind this.

Suddenly there is a terrible crash as the end of a ladder comes through the window. Debbie screams and jumps out of the way. Jatinder dives onto the floor. The whole room comes to a stop as everyone stares at the ladder. Jatinder leaps up angrily.

Jatinder   Greene! I knew it!

Mr Baxter rushes in.

Mr Baxter   What on earth is going on?

The ladder starts to move. Mr Baxter goes to the window. Outside Gary is tugging away at the ladder, which is poking through the window.

Mr Baxter   Greene, what are you doing with that ladder?

Gary   Just a slight problem, Sir.

Mr Baxter   You, Greene, are the absolute limit. You're always in trouble.

Gary	Can't help it, Sir. We've got to get Russell down, Sir.
Mr Baxter	Down? Down from where? Not on Kuriosmos, is he?
Gary	No, Sir, the roof.
Mr Baxter	I don't believe this.
Jatinder	They shouldn't have even been out here, Sir.
Mr Baxter	Well, there's no time for recriminations at the moment. Let's get Morris off that roof and on to the stage for the curtain call. The play has nearly finished.
Gary	Oh, no, Sir, my costume's all torn!

Scene Seventeen

Characters: All the pupils and teachers.

It is some minutes later and all the cast are on stage. Gary is at the back because of his torn costume. The musicians play a few more bars and then the cast breaks out into cheering and waving and the audience applauds enthusiastically. They take three bows and when the noise dies down they beckon the backstage crew on to the stage. Lisa pushes Carlton on in his wheelchair.

| Jatinder | Thanks, everyone. Thank you. |

The applauding and cheering stops.

We really hope you've enjoyed our performance tonight. Before you go we'd like to give our thanks to the teachers who were responsible for putting on this production. Without them there would have been no school play.

Everybody cheers.

Jatinder   So first, we'd like to thank Mr Baxter.

Mr Baxter walks on to the stage to more cheers and is given a card and a bottle wrapped in gift paper. The audience and cast applaud.

Jatinder   Second, our Director of Music, Miss Solomons.

Miss Solomons comes shyly on stage. The musicians strike a few chords on their instruments and cheer and whoop. She is handed a bouquet of flowers and a card. The audience and cast applaud.

Jatinder   And last but not least, our very own Ms Strange. She has worked tirelessly and overcome smashed scenery, broken legs, and last but not least a ladder through a window – which you might just have heard this evening.

The audience laughs.

But despite all this she's put on a fantastic production! Miss, where are you?

Ms Strange walks on stage and bedlam erupts. She is given a bouquet and card and the Hall and stage are ringing with applause. Gradually they calm down but then there are several cries of 'Speech'. *Ms Strange holds up her hand for quiet and the Hall is hushed.*

Ms Strange   Thank you, Jatinder, for those very kind words. Last year, after my first school production I swore never to be involved in another one again.

Mock boos.

And yet here I am.

Cheers.

But this time I mean it. Never again!

The cast whoops and yells.

Ms Strange   However, I can't bow out without thanking all of you

who have been involved in this play. To the CDT
staff who with a willing band of helpers gave many
hours of their free time to build and erect the
scenery. To Mr Baxter, whose help with rehearsals
was indispensable, and to Miss Solomons and all
the musicians whose live and recorded music was
essential to this production. To the backstage crew,
lighting, sound, and props, who achieved such a
high standard under the leadership of Jatinder. To
the cast, all of whom were wonderful and so
enthusiastic. I don't usually single out anyone but a
special mention has to be made for someone who
stepped in at the last minute when our lead singer
broke his leg only a few days before the first
performance – Gary Greene.

More whoops and yells.

Ms Strange   Gary was bitterly disappointed when he was told he
couldn't do this part because he was not old
enough, so it's ironic that he ended up giving a
superb performance as the pop star after all. And
from what I've heard this evening, he's been further
involved in climbing up the ladder of success!

Everyone cheers.

Lisa   Yeah, even I thought he was quite good.
Gary   Cor!
Ms Strange   And if I hadn't seen Carlton's fall with my own eyes I
might have suspected foul play.

Everyone laughs.

Ms Strange   He stepped in at very short notice and carried off
the part very well. Thank you, Gary.

Everyone applauds.

Gary   Cor, did you hear that? Did you hear what Miss said?
Cool!
Russell   Yes, but just wait till Monday. The Caretaker's going
to go ape.

Ms Strange speaks to the audience.

Ms Strange But now it's time for you to go home and for us to let our hair down and have our party. Goodnight, everybody.

There is more cheering and the audience leaves. Gradually those on stage break up.

Karen Well done, Gary.

Rina Yes, Miss was right. Well done.

Gary Thanks.

Rina Where's Debbie?

Karen Here she comes.

Debbie Oh! Carlton's just said how good I was and he held my hand.

Karen Better not wash for a week then.

Gary Nah, better watch out going home. Lisa Romero might jump out at you.

Rina Don't be silly, Gary.

Debbie No, actually she said well done too, although she made sure she stood close to Carlton and put her arm round his shoulder whilst she said it. I don't know what she thought I'd do. Kidnap him in his wheelchair!

Gary Yeah, we could have run off with him down the road like in a chariot race.

Rina Gary!

Karen She's changed her tune. She was threatening to see you off you last time.

Debbie I think Miss had a word with her.

Gary Come on, girls, that's enough talking. They're putting the grub and the drinks out and I'm starving.

Karen What's new?

They all laugh.

The End

Good Friends

Mollie Hemens

List of Characters

Pupils
Daniel
Gary
Karen
Debbie
David
Peter
Pupils 1–6

Parents
Mrs Smith (Daniel's Mum)
Mrs Greene (Gary's Mum)
Mrs Carrington (Mrs C. – Debbie's Mum)
Mr Carrington (Mr C. – Debbie's Dad)

Others
Shopkeeper

Teachers
Ms Strange, English and Drama
Mrs Davies, Head of English
Mr Bourne, Art

GOOD FRIENDS

Scene One

Characters: Daniel, Gary, Karen, Debbie, David, Peter, Mr Bourne.

A rainy morning in February. 7S are beginning an Art lesson with Mr Bourne.

Mr Bourne   All right, all right you lot, let's have a bit of quiet. No, Smith, don't put your rotten wet bag on the nice clean pile of paper. What am I doing, I ask myself? I'm wasted, some of you haven't got the sense you were born with.

He raises his voice.

I said, quiet!

The class starts to settle down.

That's better. Now, where was I?

Debbie   Sir, I haven't got my Art homework book. I was in a rush this morning and Mum said …

Mr Bourne   (*interrupting*) Don't bother me now, there's a good girl, you won't be needing your book today.

He addresses the class

Now, I am waiting. I could grow old waiting.

Daniel speaks privately to Gary.

Daniel   Well, don't hold your breath, he's got to be 103 if he's a day! My uncle said he was here when he came to this school and he's got a baby.

Gary   Mr Bourne's got a baby? He can't have, he's too old and he's a bloke.

Daniel	No, you dork. My uncle's girlfriend's got a baby and my uncle used to…
Mr Bourne	Smith, why is it that when everyone else can understand plain English, you can't? Why are you talking? (*sarcastically*) Do tell us, don't keep your gems of wit and wisdom for Greene's ears alone. Well, are you ready for me to start the lesson?
Daniel	(*muttering*) Yes, Sir.
Mr Bourne	What's that? I can't hear you.
Daniel	(*louder*) Yes, Sir.
Mr Bourne	Right, I want you all to think a bit more about the still life drawings you were doing last week. Karen and Debbie, give the work out please. Now you know where everything is, no water, no paints, no glue, no scissors. You can use pencil, felt tip, crayon, or charcoal. No noise, no mess, no arguments, and we'll all get on very well together. Jump to it!

The pupils begin to organise themselves.

Karen	Here's your drawing, Gary.
Gary	Thanks.
Daniel	I hate him, Bourne, he thinks he's it. He's always having a go at me.
Karen	That's not true. You wind him up, you draw attention to yourself.
Gary	How do you draw attention?
Karen } **Daniel** }	Shut up!

Karen speaks to Daniel.

Karen	I mean it, you should try keeping your mouth shut once in a while, don't get yourself noticed.
Daniel	It's all right for you, you're a girl. He likes girls. If that had been me forgetting my homework book instead of Debbie it would have been four detentions, a million lines and an ear bashing.

Debbie joins the group.

Debbie I thought you didn't do homework, I thought you were the hard man.

Daniel Yeah, well you know what I mean.

Mr Bourne Right, you lot, quiet and you might learn something.

Daniel speaks privately to Gary.

Daniel Oh no, not again. Does he like the sound of his own voice or what?

Mr Bourne The Rotary Club have announced an Art Competition. The title is 'My Life.' You have to get together a mini-exhibition representing somebody's life. It can be paintings, drawings, photographs, models, etc. The closing date is the end of this term, so you've got about six weeks and there are cash prizes. That should interest you lot. The first prize is £50 and there are two runners up prizes of £20 each.

David Does it have to be our life or somebody else's?

Mr Bourne Either.

David Are we allowed to use the Art Room at break times?

Mr Bourne The usual rules apply. If you are a member of Art Club, yes; if not, no.

David speaks to Peter.

David We're allowed. I'll meet you here straight after the lunch bell.

Peter Great, I've got an idea already.

Daniel sarcastically imitates David.

Daniel 'We're allowed, we're allowed.' Wimp!

He turns to the others.

That rules out about half the world. Old Bourney has got his favourites and if you're not one of them you can kiss that competition goodbye. Not that I want to enter it anyway, it's for wimps and girls.

Gary You can always be born again.

The others look at him witheringly.

Get it? *Bourne again!*

Debbie Gary, I swear, one more feeble joke, just one more and I'll …

Daniel (*interrupting*) And you'll what? Go on, tell us.

Karen Leave her. If you want to pick on somebody pick on me.

Daniel Ooh, Mrs Hard Woman. I suppose you're going to enter this competition then, seeing as you're in Art Club and you're teacher's pet.

Karen As a matter of fact you've got quite a talent yourself, only you choose not to use it. Doing well at school is for boffs and we all know that the great Daniel Smith is not a boff. He may be a know-it-all idiot, but he's not a boff.

Daniel (*angrily*) Leave it out, you don't know anything about me.

Karen Well, I know about that Art Competition you won in the Juniors and I know about how you were chosen to do the school Christmas card when you were seven.

Gary Were you? I never knew that. What did you draw?

Daniel Your teeth from your gums if you don't shut up.

Debbie Why don't you come to Art Club with us and enter the competition? You never know, you might win the £50.

Daniel £50? That's pathetic! My uncle has just bought a state-of-the-art camera, wide-angle and zoom for £450 and I can use it any time. £50 won't buy you anything.

Karen Oh, yes?

Daniel Oh, yeah.

Gary Oh, yeah.

Karen
Daniel } Shut up!

Karen   Prove it then, borrow your uncle's camera, take
some pictures and come to Art Club. I'll show you
how to develop them. It'll have to be a black and
white film though, we can't do colour.

Gary   Your big chance, boy. A lunchtime to remember in
the dark room with Karen.

Karen and Daniel both go to hit Gary, who ducks
away.

Karen
Daniel } Shut up!

Scene Two

Characters: Ms Strange, Mrs Davies, Mr Bourne.

Two weeks later at lunchtime in the Staffroom. Mr
Bourne is eating a sandwich and doing the
crossword. Ms Strange is marking a pile of exercise
books. Mrs Davies enters.

Mrs Davies   Well, well, Norman, you certainly seem to be the
flavour of the month. What's the big attraction in
that Art Room of yours?

Mr Bourne   Sarcasm will get you nowhere.

Mrs Davies   I'm being serious. It seemed as if there was a Year
Seven reunion going on.

Mr Bourne looks up from his newspaper.

Mr Bourne   What? There shouldn't be more than six of them in
there at a time. (*sighing*) I suppose I'll have to go
and check up on them.

Mrs Davies   They were okay, a bit noisy and a few more than six I'd say, but they were okay. What's the big attraction anyway?

Mr Bourne   (*grumpily*) It's this Art Competition. 'My Life.' It wasn't my idea in the first place. I had my arm twisted by the Head, who thought it would be good publicity for the school. Let her organise it, that's what I say. I thought I was here to teach, not to baby mind in my lunch hour.

Mrs Davies   (*smiling*) You know you love it really. I was surprised to see Daniel Smith though. I didn't think he was interested in anything that we had to offer.

Ms Strange looks up.

Ms Strange   Yes, have you seen his camera? He was showing it off in Registration. I told him that it was too expensive for him to be trailing around school. I even offered to look after it for him till the end of the day, but he said he would look after it himself. I just hope it's insured. Do you think I should phone his parents?

Mr Bourne   It's none of your business. If the parents let him have such expensive toys it's down to them.

Ms Strange   It's hardly a toy. Still, perhaps I'll have another word with him.

Mr Bourne   You won't get any thanks for interfering. I'd better go and have a look at what they're up to in the Art Room.

He puts his newspaper down and reluctantly gets up out of his chair.

Don't let anyone do any clues whilst I'm gone.

Mr Bourne exits.

Mrs Davies   It certainly makes a change to see Norman working his lunch hour. I hope he doesn't overdo it, he might get too tired.

Scene Three

Characters: Daniel, Gary, Karen, Debbie.

Later that day. Daniel, Gary, Karen and Debbie are walking home from school. They stop outside a parade of shops. Daniel puts his schoolbag down, carefully opens it and takes out the camera.

Gary   (*pleadingly*) Let me have a hold.

Daniel   Drop dead.

Karen   A nice way to talk to your best friend, I'm sure. Go on, it wouldn't hurt you to let him hold it.

Daniel   Mind your own business. The day you've got a camera like this is the day you can decide who uses it and who doesn't.

Gary   I didn't say I wanted to use it, I just want a hold.

Karen   You want all the favours, don't you, and you give nothing back. Who is it who's going to develop and print this film for you?

Daniel   All right, Mrs Generosity Plus, stop fussing.

Debbie   Pack it in you two, you're always having a go at each other.

Daniel   (*grinning*) We like it really, don't we, Karrie baby?

Daniel puts his arm around Karen's shoulder and tries to kiss her cheek.

Karen   (*aggressively*) Get off!

Debbie   I just hope Mr Bourne doesn't notice that he's missing a black-and-white film.

Daniel   No, there were loads of them on his desk.

Karen   Mr Bourne would have put those films out ready for his exam class.

Daniel   He's not going to miss one film, it's not as if it cost a lot. I bet he gets a good discount. They're hard to get hold of over the counter. It's all colour these days.

Karen   That's not the point, it doesn't belong to us.

Daniel   Listen to Miss Goody Goody, will you. Who's going to tell Boring Bourney, you?

He speaks in a simpering high-pitched voice.

'Oh, Mr Bourne, Sir. Please, Sir. My friend Daniel helped himself to one of your black-and-white films. And by the way, Sir, I'm in some of the photos he took.'

Karen   (*uncomfortable*) Well ...

Gary   Come on, Karen, forget about it. It would have been hard for Daniel to get hold of a film from a shop. He would have had to go all the way into town. I wish I'd never mentioned wanting to hold the stupid camera now.

Daniel   Okay, you lot, let's have one for the album.

He busily organises the others into a group ready to take a photo.

Daniel   Move back, I can't get your legs in.

Debbie   If we move back any more, we'll go through the shop window. You move back. Anyway, I hate my legs, just take the top half.

Karen   (*sarcastically*) Call yourself a photographer. I thought that camera was supposed to be state of the art.

Daniel moves back until he is standing in the gutter. A passing motorist sounds her horn and he jumps back on to the pavement. At last he is ready.

Daniel   Smile, please.

The others freeze and smile. The picture is taken.

Karen   I'm glad that's over. Though what it's got to do with 'My Life,' I don't know. Come on, Debbie, I've got to get back for my tea.

The two girls saunter off together. Daniel shouts after them.

Daniel We all have to start somewhere. I'm just practising, aren't I? Stupid women!

Scene Four

Characters: Daniel, Gary, Shopkeeper.

Daniel and Gary enter the newsagent's. Daniel has the camera slung over his shoulder.

Shopkeeper That's a nice camera you've got there.

Daniel What?

Shopkeeper The camera, it's a bit smart. I know a bit about cameras. Is it yours? Mind if I have a look?

Daniel Yeah, take a look.

He hands the camera over to the shopkeeper, who examines it carefully.

It's not mine, it belongs to my uncle, I'm just borrowing it.

Shopkeeper It's worth a bob or two. You're a lucky lad, you've got a generous uncle.

Daniel Yeah, well.

He pauses, as if thinking to himself.

I borrowed it for a project we're doing at school about people in the community. You know, Social Education and all that.

Gary looks surprised. Daniel grins at him and winks.

He turns back to the Shopkeeper.

Daniel   Can my friend take a picture of you at work for our project?

He hands the camera to Gary who can hardly believe his luck.

Gary   Wow, thanks! Are you sure?

Daniel   Go on, have a go. It's easy, you can't go wrong, the camera does it all for you. Just look through here and gently press the button …

Shopkeeper   (*interrupting*) Come on, come on, I haven't got all day.

Gary   Okay, okay.

Gary and the Shopkeeper busy themselves with the taking of the photographs. They do not notice Daniel, who takes advantage of the situation to stuff his pockets quickly with anything he can grab from the sweets display. He turns back to them, just as Gary finishes taking a photograph.

Daniel   (*grinning*) Told you it was easy.

Shopkeeper   Don't forget to come back and show me the pictures.

Gary   We will, thanks.

Outside, on the pavement, Gary hands the camera back to Daniel.

Daniel   How many did you take?

Gary   About six, was that okay?

Daniel   (*triumphantly*) Beat you! I took more than that!

Gary   What?

Daniel pulls a handful of sweets and chocolate from each pocket.

Gary   (*shocked*) What's that lot?

Daniel   What's it look like? Haven't you seen sweets before?

He opens his bag and empties the contents of his pockets into it.

Here, pick a bar, any bar.

Gary   (*still shocked*) I don't know.

Daniel   Come on, you're hungry, aren't you?

Gary nods.

Then stop being such a wimp.

Gary shrugs his shoulders. He chooses a chocolate bar and starts to eat it.

Daniel   (*smiling*) That's better – we're partners, you and me.

Scene Five

Characters: Daniel, Gary, Karen, Debbie, David, Peter, Mr Bourne.

The next day at lunchtime in the Art Room. Karen, Debbie, David and Peter are working on their Art projects. Mr Bourne enters the room.

Mr Bourne   My, my, aren't we busy little beavers? This is what I like to see. Anybody need any help?

Peter   No thanks, Sir, we're okay, aren't we, David?

David nods. He is drawing an arrangement of his football kit.

Mr Bourne   Good. By the way, I'm not happy about the number of people who have been in here at lunchtimes. They can't all be members of Art Club.

Debbie   It's the competition, Sir. Quite a few kids have wanted to enter.

Mr Bourne   Well, it's quiet enough now, perhaps they've lost interest. I'm putting you in charge, Karen. If you get any problems come and tell me. I'll be in the Staffroom.

Karen Yes, Sir.

Mr Bourne starts to leave the room. Karen calls after him.

Oh, Sir. Would it be all right if I went into the stock cupboard to get some more acrylic paint? The container is almost empty.

Mr Bourne Yes, fine. You know where it is, it's right at the back, next to the boxes of brushes. Here, you'll need the key.

He hands her a bunch of keys.

It's this one with the red tag. Let me have them back at the end of lunch and make sure you lock the cupboard up again before you leave the room.

Karen Yes, sir. Thanks, Sir.

Mr Bourne leaves the room. Karen unlocks the door of the stock cupboard (offstage) and goes in. Daniel and Gary enter the Art Room noisily singing a football chant.

Daniel ⎫ (*together*) Here we go, here we go, here we go,
Gary ⎭ here we go, here we go, here we go-oh.

Daniel speaks to the others.

Daniel Watch ya! How's it going?

Debbie It was going fine till you two hooligans arrived.

Daniel Do you hear that, Gary? I don't think she is happy to see us.

Daniel moves about the room looking at the various displays. He stops at David's table. Debbie speaks to Gary.

Debbie What are you two doing here anyway?

Gary It was really boring in the playground. The Year

Nines have taken up all the room as usual, so we thought we'd come and annoy you.

Daniel Yeah, and I want to talk to Karen about developing my film. She said she would. Where is she anyway?

Peter She's in the stock cupboard.

Daniel Thanks, mate.

He strolls over to the stock cupboard, calling to Karen as he goes.

Oh, Karrie, light of my life, can you do me a really special favour?

David He's a right one.

Gary You can say that again.

David He's a ...

Debbie (*interrupting*) Pack it in, you two. Some of us have got work to do. Anyway, Gary, you and Daniel aren't supposed to be in here. You're not members of Art Club and Mr Bourne is clamping down.

Gary (*wheedling*) Come on, Debbie, you know you like us really.

Debbie Well, now you're here, you may as well make yourself useful. Hold this bit of card down for me.

Debbie turns back to her model. Gary obediently holds down the piece of card.

Gary I get all the good jobs. Just don't get any glue on my hands, I like to keep them nice and clean.

Scene Six

Characters: Daniel, Karen.

In the stock cupboard Karen is sorting out a pile of paper and card. Daniel enters. He trips over some packs of paper that are on the floor and bumps into Karen.

Karen   Daniel!

Daniel   Sorry, it wasn't my fault! This place is a mess, there's stuff all over the floor. What's this lot then?

Daniel starts to fiddle with some boxes that are stacked on a shelf.

Karen   Leave them alone. If you break something, you'll get me into trouble. You're not even supposed to be in the Art Room, let alone in here.

Daniel   I was wondering if you had time to develop my film for me.

Karen   I can't do it today, I'm not sure when Mr Bourne will let me use the darkroom. I'll ask him and let you know.

Daniel nods his agreement.

Can you do me a favour and move these boxes of paint over into that corner?

Daniel moves the boxes. At the back of the shelf, there is a jar that has been hidden by the boxes. It has some money in it.

Daniel   What's this money for?

Daniel picks up the jar, takes the money out and starts to count it.

Karen   Put it back! Why can't you leave things alone? It's most probably the money that Mr Bourne charges for developing and materials and stuff.

Daniel Do you mean he makes you pay? What a fiddle, it should be free. There must be about twenty quid here.

Karen It's not his money, idiot brain. It goes back to the school. Why should the school have to pay for everything anyway? Come on, put that money back. I've wasted enough time. I need to get back to work.

Scene Seven

Characters: Daniel, Gary, Karen, Debbie, David, Peter.

In the Art Room, Gary is helping Debbie. David and Peter are working on their projects. Daniel puts his bag on a table and takes out his camera. He puts the camera down near the edge of the table next to the bag. Karen resumes work on her project.

Peter Nice camera.

Daniel is pleased. He rummages around in his bag and pulls out several chocolate bars. He speaks to Peter.

Daniel Want one? What do you fancy? Go on, choose any of 'em. You too, Dave.

David David, my name is David.

Daniel Ooh, David! Not too posh, are we, to have one of my Mars Bars? Go on, they're free samples. There's loads more where these came from, eh, Gary?

Daniel looks across at Gary who sniggers. Gary,

David and Peter crowd round and the boys choose a chocolate bar each. Gary talks with his mouth full of chocolate.

Gary Come on, girls, you don't know what you're missing. Break your diets for once and live dangerously.

Karen Shut up, pea brain. We don't all want to be spotty pigs.

Peter I wouldn't take that if I were you, Gary.

Gary Let's get 'em, then!

Peter and Gary chase the girls around the room. They laugh and shriek and dodge around the tables. Daniel joins in. He throws David's football across the room to Gary.

Daniel Here, Gary, catch!

Gary turns round just in time to catch the ball and hurls it back. Daniel stretches to catch it. He manages to touch it with his finger tips. The ball drops heavily on to the table next to the camera, which is knocked to the floor. There is a sudden silence as they all look at the camera. Debbie rushes over to the camera, picks it up and examines it.

Debbie I think it's broken.

Daniel snatches the camera from her. The plastic surround of the lens is badly cracked.

Daniel speaks furiously to Gary.

Daniel Now look what you've done!

Gary sits down heavily on a chair.

Gary It wasn't my fault.

Daniel Yes, it was, you threw the ball!

Gary I did? You mean you did. You were the one who picked it up and threw it first, I was just throwing it back. Don't start having a go and blaming me.

David	Gary's right. You had no business touching the ball in the first place, Daniel.
Daniel	(*angrily*) Shut up and mind your own business! Who asked for your opinion?
Peter	Stress!
Debbie	Why can't you go to a camera shop and get it mended?
Karen	They won't be able to mend that, the plastic's cracked. You need to buy a new lens.
Daniel	Where am I supposed to get that sort of money from? A new lens is serious money.
Karen	(*patiently*) Get a secondhand one then. Anyway, it was an accident. Tell your uncle and get him to claim it on his insurance.
Daniel	(*muttering*) I don't know if he's got insurance.
Karen	What did you say?
Daniel	Nothing.

Karen shrugs her shoulders.

Karen	Oh, well, you shouldn't have been mucking about.

A bell rings

That's our lunch sitting. Coming, Debs?

Debbie	Yes.
Karen	What about you two?

Gary stands up. Daniel glares at him. Gary changes his mind and sits down again.

Daniel	I don't feel like eating.
Karen	Suit yourself. If you are staying here can you keep an eye on things for me? Mr Bourne put me in charge. I'll only be about ten minutes, okay?

Daniel nods his agreement. Karen and Debbie leave the room. Daniel speaks aggressively to David and Peter.

Daniel	What are you two staring at? Get lost! Clear off!
Peter	Stress! Come on, David, we know when we're not wanted.

Peter and David grin at each other. They saunter slowly out of the room.

Daniel	Now what am I going to do?
Gary	Claim it on the insurance like Karen said.
Daniel	It's not that simple, stupid. I don't know if my uncle's got insurance. Not that it makes any difference. He doesn't know I've used the camera, let alone brought it into school.
Gary	(*surprised*) What?
Daniel	You heard.
Gary	You mean he doesn't know you've got it?
Daniel	Totally correct, Mastermind. He's gone abroad to work for a few months and he's left some of his gear in our spare room. So I borrowed the camera.
Gary	What did you do that for? He'll do you.
Daniel	(*irritably*) Do you think I don't know that? It's stupid Karen's fault for daring me to take some photos for that stupid project. Stupid, stupid, stupid!

Daniel kicks the chair angrily.

Gary	Well, your uncle's not going to want his camera for a while so you can replace the lens.
Daniel	(*sarcastically*) And what shall I do for money, rob a bank? Hey, you've got some savings in the Building Society. How much have you got? You can lend me some.
Gary	I can't. My Mum keeps my pass book, she'd get suspicious.
Daniel	Make up an excuse for wanting the money.
Gary	Then she'll want to see what I've bought. Isn't there some way you can earn the money? Get a paper round or something?

Daniel What's all this *you* business? This is partly your fault, we're in this together. Let me think.

Daniel sits down at one of the tables and stares off into space. Gary drums his fingers on the table top.

Daniel Got it! (*urgently*) Right, listen, we haven't got much time. Old Bourney keeps a jar of money in his stock cupboard. I saw it when I was in there with Karen, must be about twenty quid. We'll use it as a float. We'll go into town and buy up a load of those twelve packs of crisps and eight packs of Mars Bars and stuff, then sell it off to the kids at school and we'll have enough to buy a secondhand lens with the profits.

Gary (*shocked*) We can't do that! We can't use that money, it's not ours.

Daniel Yes, we can. Don't you know what a float is? We'll borrow the money, just till tomorrow. Then when we've sold that lot of stuff, we'll put the money back into the jar. We then use what profit we've made to buy more stuff, sell that, and keep carrying on like that till we've got enough for a lens.

Gary (*firmly*) No, I don't want any part of it, it's stealing.

Daniel It's not stealing, it's borrowing. Stealing is taking stuff and not putting it back.

He glares menacingly.

Remember the chocolate from the shop yesterday?

Gary (*self-righteously*) That was you, not me.

Daniel Oh, it was, was it? Who was in the shop with me? Who distracted the shopkeeper's attention while I took the stuff? Who shared it with me afterwards?

Gary I didn't know what you were doing.

Daniel (*threateningly*) Prove it!

There is a silence.

Daniel (*persuasively*) Come on, Gary. We're partners, I need your help, buddy.

Gary fiddles with his tie.

Daniel You don't have to take the money. Just keep watch for me, it'll only take a few seconds. Then after school we'll go down the supermarket and buy the stuff. I'll put the money back by the end of school tomorrow, I promise. It's not stealing, just borrowing.

Gary (*reluctantly*) All right, but be quick.

Daniel breathes a sigh of relief.

Daniel That's my man. I owe you one, partner.

Daniel goes into the stock cupboard (offstage). Gary goes to the door and looks out into the corridor. He calls out to Daniel.

Gary What if Bourney notices the money's gone?

Daniel calls back from the stock cupboard.

Daniel That's a chance we'll have to take. Anyway, he won't, it's only till tomorrow.

Scene Eight

Characters: Daniel, Gary, Karen, Debbie, Pupils 1–6, Mr Bourne.

The next day in the Art Room at morning break, Daniel and Gary have set up a table near the door. There is a large quantity of packets of crisps and various chocolate bars on the table. A crowd of pupils has gathered and they are noisily pushing and shoving each other. Karen and Debbie are standing to one side watching the proceedings with amusement.

Pupil 1   Me, serve me.

Pupil 2   I was here first.

Pupil 3   Five packets of cheese and onion, one beef, two salt and vinegar.

Pupil 4   Stop pushing.

Pupil 5   Gary, serve me.

Pupil 6   Have you got any Smarties? I like Smarties.

Daniel   (*aggressively*) Get back, you lot! One at a time and stop helping yourselves.

He slaps the hand of a boy who has edged to the front and is trying to help himself, looks across at Gary and grins.

See, I told you that this lot was greedy. We'll be sold out in five minutes.

He shouts to the crowd in general.

Get back!

Mr Bourne enters the room and pushes his way angrily into the crowd.

Mr Bourne   (*shouting*) What's going on, what's all this noise about?

The pupils become silent as Mr Bourne makes his way to the table.

Mr Bourne   Smith. I should have known.

He looks down at the table full of crisps and chocolate.

What is all this lot?

Debbie   It's Gary and Daniel, Sir. They've set up a sort of tuck shop, Sir.

Mr Bourne turns and notices Karen and Debbie for the first time.

Mr Bourne   (*incredulously*) Tuck shop? I'll give you tuck shop.

He claps his hands together sharply.

Out, all of you, now! Come on, move it!

Gary and Daniel start to move from behind the table.

Mr Bourne   No, not you two. You stay where you are.

He speaks to Karen and Debbie.

You two girls as well. Everybody else, out!

The other pupils leave the room quickly, talking, laughing and grumbling amongst themselves. Mr Bourne, Gary, Daniel, Karen and Debbie remain.

Mr Bourne   Who's going to start explaining? Smith?

Daniel does not answer.

Karen, then.

Karen   It's like Debbie said, Sir. Daniel and Gary are selling chocolate and crisps.

Mr Bourne   And you just let them in here to set up shop. Didn't you try to stop them?

Karen   I couldn't, Sir.

Mr Bourne   It's you I usually leave in charge. You should have come to get me.

Karen   Yes, Sir.

Mr Bourne   Why didn't you?

Karen   I don't know, Sir.

Daniel   (*interrupting*) She didn't want to grass us up.

Mr Bourne   (*sarcastically*) *Grass us up?* What a quaint turn of phrase. I wonder where it originated. I suppose you mean that she didn't want to inform the authorities of your activities?

Gary   Yes, Sir.

Debbie   They wanted to make some money, Sir.

Daniel mutters furiously to Debbie.

Daniel   Shut up!

Mr Bourne   Oh, they did, did they? And for what purpose?

Debbie   (*mumbles*) Don't know, Sir.

Mr Bourne   I think you do, Debbie, but let's go straight to the horse's mouth. Smith, what is the meaning of all this? Collecting for charity, are we? Suddenly developed a social conscience, have we?

Daniel   No, Sir. I need some money, Sir, to buy a lens for my uncle's camera.

Mr Bourne   Ah, the famous camera. It's the talk of the Staffroom, you know. Hasn't it got a lens, because it's not much good without one, is it?

Mr Bourne smiles sarcastically.

Daniel   It got broke, Sir.

Mr Bourne   Dear, dear, and how did that happen, I wonder?

Daniel   Don't know, Sir.

Mr Bourne   (*angrily*) Don't know, don't know. That's all I seem to be hearing and I'm becoming rather bored, so if you don't mind …

Karen   (*interrupting*) We might as well tell him, he won't let up till we do. The boys were mucking about in

	the Art Room, chasing me and Debbie.
Daniel	Karen!
Gary	That's not fair.
Karen	I suppose we were all having a muck around. Daniel threw a ball, Gary threw it back and …
Mr Bourne	(*interrupting*) Yes, yes, and the camera, or rather the lens, got damaged.
Debbie	Yes, Sir.
Mr Bourne	So you decided to go into the confectionery business. Enterprising, I must say.
Debbie	Not us, Sir, Daniel and Gary. We didn't know anything about it till we got here, did we, Karen?
Karen	No.
Mr Bourne	Where did you get the chocolate and crisps from?
Daniel	From the supermarket, those big packs you can buy.
Mr Bourne	That must have cost you a pretty penny. Where did you get the money from to buy it all in the first place?

There is silence.

Mr Bourne	I'm waiting.

The pupils do not answer.

Do your parents know about this?

Daniel and Gary look at each other uncomfortably.

Mr Bourne	(*slowly*) I see. I think that a phone call is in order.
Gary	(*anxiously*) Please don't, Sir! My Mum will kill me!
Mr Bourne	I don't see that I have much choice, Greene. Your parents place you in our care during the school day so they have a right to know if things aren't quite as they seem. What if they found out about this little enterprise of yours? They would be within their rights to make a formal complaint to the Head. I have no choice because, much as I admire your plan of raising the money for the lens, I can't have

any part in it unless I know the whole story.

He looks at Karen and Debbie.

Girls?

Debbie I don't know anything about it, Sir, honest.

Karen Me neither, the first I knew about it was when I came into the Art Room.

Mr Bourne Boys?

There is silence.

Mr Bourne shrugs his shoulders.

Mr Bourne You're not doing yourselves any favours by not telling me, I've got to report this matter to the Head of Year, anyway. People are always more inclined to treat you favourably if you tell them the whole story. I must admit, I'm quite amused by your fund-raising idea, though why you couldn't have told your parents about the lens being broken, Smith, I don't know. You've certainly found a complicated solution to your problem.

Mr Bourne loses patience.

Okay, I will have to phone your parents. Get this lot cleared up and then come with me to the Year Head's office.

Mr Bourne starts to leave the room. Gary hastily calls after him.

Gary Daniel couldn't tell his parents 'cos they don't know he's borrowed the camera.

Daniel *(furiously)* Shut up!

Gary We have to tell him. If all this gets back to my Mum, I'm dead!

He speaks in a rush.

He wanted me to get the money from the Building Society, but I couldn't do that. He said we were only borrowing, you know, a float. He said we would put the money back today.

Daniel glares at Gary, appalled.

Mr Bourne   Slow down. What float? What money?

Gary   The money in your jar in the stock cupboard.

Daniel is absolutely furious.

Daniel   You fool, now you've gone and done it! He'll tell your Mum anyway!

Mr Bourne   You mean to say you helped yourselves. (*pause*) How did you ... ?

He looks at Karen, suddenly realising.

Karen   (*panicking*) I had nothing to do with it, Sir! I didn't know, honestly!

Daniel   She knew nothing about it, it was my idea.

Mr Bourne speaks to Karen.

Mr Bourne   But you had the key. You were in charge and I trusted you. This is one for the Head. Fooling about is one thing. Theft is another. Come on, I'll lock this room up just as it is and escort you lot to the Head's Office.

Debbie   Not me, Sir, I'm not involved.

Mr Bourne   Don't play the innocent with me, Missie. You as well.

Scene Nine

Characters: Daniel, Gary, Karen, Debbie, Ms Strange.

The same day, in the afternoon. Daniel and Debbie are waiting outside the Head's office.

Debbie It's not fair. I shouldn't have to see the Head, I wasn't involved at all.

Daniel Well, you're here now so there's not a lot you can do about it. Did you give Ms Strange your written statement?

Debbie Yes.

Daniel What did you put?

Debbie I'm not telling *you*. If it wasn't for *you* I wouldn't be standing outside the Head's office.

Daniel You didn't mind having your photo taken, did you?

Debbie How was I supposed to know that you didn't have permission to use the camera? You told us that ...

Daniel (*interrupting*) I know, I know, don't keep on. I'm in enough trouble.

Debbie What do you think they'll do to us?

Daniel You'll be all right, you didn't do anything, or so you keep reminding me.

Debbie Is your Mum coming up to the school?

Daniel Don't know. Ms Strange couldn't get through when she telephoned earlier. She said she'd keep trying. What about your Mum?

Debbie Yes, she'll be here soon. I expect my Dad will come as well. He's on the late shift this week so he would have been at home when they telephoned.

Daniel He's a copper, 'aint he? Can't say as I'd like having a copper for a Dad.

Debbie (*offended*) He hasn't got two heads, you know. He's just ordinary like everybody else's Dad. I wonder where Gary and Karen are. They must be writing a lot. They've been ages.

Daniel   If Gary had kept his big mouth shut in the first place, we wouldn't be in this mess. He didn't have to tell Bourney about borrowing the money, nobody need ever have known. I would've thought of some excuse or another about how we could afford to buy all the crisps and stuff.

Ms Strange comes out of the Head's office.

Ms Strange   Well, you two, Mrs MacDonald has got your statements. I'm just going to get Karen and Gary, then I'll go to the Entrance Hall to wait for your parents. Both your parents will be here, Debbie, and just your mother, Daniel. We managed to get through to her in the end. You shouldn't have to wait too much longer.

Daniel   Good, we've been here ages.

Ms Strange   I don't think that's the correct attitude, Daniel. I need hardly remind you of the seriousness of the situation. If I were in your shoes, I would be polite and careful not to say anything that might make matters worse. I'm going to get Karen and Gary now. I'll be back soon. In the meantime, think about what you are going to say and how you are going to behave during your interviews.

Ms Strange goes.

Daniel   'If I were in your shoes.' Teachers, they're all the same!

Debbie   She's only trying to tell you for your own good.

Daniel   You sound just like my Mum, that's what she'd say.

Ms Strange returns with Karen and Gary.

Daniel   Here are the others. You two took your time, were you writing a book?

Gary   There was a lot to put down.

He turns to Ms Strange.

Does it matter about spelling, Miss?

Ms Strange No, Gary, the important thing is to have written the truth. I'm going to the Entrance Hall, your parents should be arriving shortly and I want to be there to meet them. Your mother will be along later, Karen. She'd had to arrange cover for her classes and she's got further to travel than the others.

Ms Strange goes.

Daniel That's a stroke of luck, Karen.

Karen You're so stupid. I'll have to face my Mum eventually. I feel really bad about all this. I hate having to cause her so much upset, she's got enough to cope with. I wish I'd never left you in the Art Room with the cupboard unlocked. I thought I could trust you.

Daniel What did you write in your statement?

Debbie Don't tell him, Karen, it's none of his business.

Karen I've got nothing to hide. I wrote the truth, about how the lens got broken and that I had asked him to keep an eye on things while we went to lunch. It was just as much of a surprise to me as it was to Mr Bourne to find out that he'd helped himself to the money that was in the cupboard. What I can't understand is why you went along with him, Gary.

Daniel None of your business.

Karen Let Gary speak for himself, for a change.

Debbie Yes, why did you go along with him, Gary?

Gary Well, he's my mate, we're partners.

Karen You're pathetic! I suppose you'd jump from the roof if he told you to. You deserve all you get.

Gary (*irritated*) You don't know anything, so shut up! I had my reasons and they're none of your business.

Daniel (*approvingly*) That's telling her.

He hesitates.

You, er, didn't write anything in your statement, you know, about the reasons?

Gary No, relax.

Debbie I don't know what you two are on about but all I can say is that you've got a good mate. It's obvious that Gary is covering for you.

Daniel Yeah, well. Did anybody mention where we got the film from?

Karen Me? It was nothing to do with any of us but since you asked, I didn't.

Debbie Me neither.

Gary Nor me. Why are you checking out our statements?

Daniel So we can get our stories straight for when we're interviewed. I bet they interview us separately with just our parents there.

Gary Oh, no. My Mum will kill me.

Debbie Here's Ms Strange.

Ms Strange returns.

Ms Strange Your parents, except for your mother, Karen, are waiting in Reception. I'll take you to join them and you will be called for your interviews with the Head separately.

Daniel Told you so.

Scene Ten

*Characters: Daniel, Gary, Karen, Debbie,
Ms Strange, Mrs Smith, Mrs Greene, Mrs Carrington,
Mr Carrington.*

*In Reception a few minutes later. The parents are
sitting in silence. Ms Strange and the pupils enter.*

Mr Carrington stands up.

Mr C. Debbie, what's been going on? What's happened?
What's all this about money having been stolen?

Mrs C. Calm down, Barry, give the girl a chance to sit down
at least.

Mrs Greene Gary, come over here!

Gary walks over to join his mother.

Gary I can explain, Mum.

Mrs Greene Sit down and shut up! You're not saying anything in
front of an audience, you'll wait until we get into the
Head Teacher's office.

Gary But, Mum …

Mrs Greene Don't 'Mum' me! Sit down and shut up! Just you
wait till I get you home, my lad!

Gary obeys his mother.

Daniel speaks to Ms Strange.

Daniel Who's going to be interviewed first, Miss?

Ms Strange I'm not sure, Daniel.

Mrs Greene I don't think it should be you. You were the one
who caused all the trouble in the first place, if what
your teacher told me on the phone is anything to go
by.

Mrs Smith jumps angrily to her feet.

Mrs Smith   Who do you think you're talking to? My Daniel might
               be no angel but he's entitled to a hearing and it's
               the teachers' job to do that, not yours.

Ms Strange   I think we should all try to remain calm. I know
               you're upset, Mrs Greene, but maybe you should
               wait for your interview with the Head.

Mr C.   I agree. From what my wife was told on the phone,
               it all sounds very complicated.

Debbie   I didn't do anything, Dad, honest.

Mr C.   I believe you, Princess, don't you worry. I've got a
               few questions myself to ask about how this matter
               has been handled but I shall wait until we talk to
               Mrs MacDonald.

Ms Strange   If you'll excuse me a moment, I'll go and see if the
               Head is ready for you.

               *Ms Strange goes. Mrs Smith and Mr Carrington
               return to their seats. Everyone sits in silence. A few
               moments later, Ms Strange returns.*

Ms Strange   Mrs MacDonald is ready for you now. She will see
               Mr and Mrs Carrington and Debbie first.

Karen   Good luck, Debbie.

Debbie   Thanks.

Ms Strange   If you'd like to come with me, I'll take you through.

Scene Eleven

Characters: Ms Strange, Mrs Davies, Mr Bourne.

The next day, in the Staffroom. School has finished for the day. Mrs Davies and Ms Strange are sitting down, drinking coffee.

Mrs Davies That's it for another day, thank goodness. I don't know if I'm coming or going this week. I'm on a course at the Teachers' Centre and, whilst it's nice to keep up with the latest developments, I feel as if I'm out of touch with what's happening back at base.

Ms Strange Oh, I don't know, I could do with some time away from the little dears, especially with the drama of the last twenty-four hours. Honestly, you wouldn't believe it. I've been heavily involved because Daniel and friends are in my form, so not only have I had a full teaching day but I've also had to be polite to irate parents.

Mrs Davies I've missed all this. I caught a snippet of gossip this morning before school, when I popped in to collect the material for the course. What's the latest storm in a teacup?

Ms Strange (*smiling*) It's more than a teacup's worth, I can tell you. It's more like a huge great mugful. I feel really sorry for Norman, although he's only got himself to blame in a way.

Mrs Davies Why?

Ms Strange It seems that young Daniel was the ringleader in a money-making enterprise designed to pay for replacing the lens on that expensive camera he's been wandering about with. The little treasures broke it in a let's-muck-about-in-the-Art-Room session.

Mrs Davies So what did they do?

Ms Strange	They bought crisps and chocolate in bulk from the supermarket and sold them off at mark-up prices. Nice theory, the only problem was that they had no start-up capital. So they helped themselves to some money that Norman keeps in a jar in his stock cupboard.
Mrs Davies	Why has he got money lying around where the kids can get at it?
Ms Strange	You tell me. He says it's money the pupils pay him for extra materials and so forth. I don't know why he doesn't keep it in the school safe.
Mrs Davies	Who else was involved?
Ms Strange	Gary Greene, Debbie Carrington and Karen Millhouse.
Mrs Davies	(*surprised*) Debbie and Karen? Gary, well, yes, he's daft enough to go along with anything his hero Daniel suggests. But Debbie and Karen, I'm amazed.
Ms Strange	It was Gary who cracked first and blew the whistle. Apparently the boys thought it up and they admit that. They say the girls weren't involved.
Mrs Davies	Why didn't the Head let the girls off?
Ms Strange	Debbie was, but not Karen. It seems that Norman had left her in charge in the Art Room and he'd also left the keys to the stock cupboard with her. Mrs MacDonald said that she should not have gone to lunch and left the cupboard open because she had been placed in a position of responsibility.
Mrs Davies	What? Oh dear, what on earth was Norman thinking of?
	Mr Bourne enters the Staffroom unnoticed. He overhears their conversation.
Ms Strange	Yes, that's the line that the parents took in the interviews. Also, Mrs Smith was furious that we hadn't informed her that Daniel had the camera in school. As if it's our responsibility.
Mrs Davies	Has the Head seen Norman?
Ms Strange	Yes, but he hasn't made any comment on the

outcome. He's walking around like a bear with a sore head.

Mrs Davies   I should think he is. Leaving money lying around and letting pupils have keys, not to mention allowing them into the Art Room unsupervised.

Mr Bourne   (*bitterly*) We all know whose side you are on.

Mrs Davies   (*embarrassed*) Norman, I didn't see you there.

Mr Bourne   Obviously. There are two sides to every story you know. The cupboard was locked most of the time and I've been keeping money in that jar for years. I had every reason to suppose I could trust Karen Millhouse. To be fair to her, she wasn't to know that Smith would help himself the minute her back was turned.

Mrs Davies   True, but at the end of the day the teacher in charge has to take responsibility.

Mr Bourne   Tell me about it. I mean, are we answerable for every single minute of every school day? That Smith boy is an idiot. He says he didn't see it as stealing, he just got himself into a mess and made it worse when he tried to get out of it. How he expected to put the money back into the jar is anybody's guess. He was bound to get found out in the end. In many ways I'm glad I caught them in the act.

Ms Strange   I wouldn't like to be in their shoes at home. Daniel has still got to face the music over the broken camera, and we all know how tough Gary's mum is on her children. That's why he cracked in the end. He's absolutely terrified of his Mum, and I can't say that I blame him!

Mrs Davies   How did the interviews go?

Ms Strange   Reasonably well, I thought. I admire the Head's diplomatic skills. Mr Carrington raised some difficult issues about supervision and how much responsibility pupils should be given. Mrs Smith was really upset, not just about Daniel being the ringleader but about what she's going to say to her brother, you know, about the camera. Mrs Millhouse finally arrived at about half past four. She was clearly upset but she was very supportive of Karen and felt that Norman had expected too much of her. I must say, they seem to have a good relationship, Karen and her mother. As for Mrs Greene, the wind was taken out of her sails completely once Mrs MacDonald had explained the extent of Gary's involvement. He really is very stupid to be so completely at Daniel's beck and call. I can't understand why he agreed to the plan.

Mrs Davies   It remains to be seen whether their friendship survives or not.

Ms Strange stands up.

Ms Strange   It all seems to be sorted out now. Mrs MacDonald has decided not to call the police in, so young Daniel has been given a second chance. He and Gary have been put on Work and Attitude Report and the money from the Art Room has been replaced. The rest of their profit, not that there was a lot, has gone to charity. Oxfam, I think.

Mr Bourne   They should have been suspended. As it is, Karen Millhouse has got away with a flea in her ear. And how seriously do you think the boys will take this being on Report business? None of them is welcome back in my Art Room. In fact, I've closed down Art Club altogether. I'm not prepared to give up all my spare time supervising the so and so's. If the Head wants Art competitions, she can organise them. These kids are supposed to be nearly young adults, or so they tell me. We should be able to trust them, not watch them every minute of the day.

Mrs Davies   It will all blow over.

She stands up.

I've got to go, it's the last day of my course tomorrow and then back to the real world. I'll see you on Monday. Have a good weekend, Norman, try not to dwell on it all too much. 'Bye.

Mrs Davies leaves the stage.

Ms Strange   I have to be going too, Norman. I'm really sorry all this happened. Maybe I should have telephoned Daniel's mother when I first saw that camera in school. But how was I to know? She might have seen it as interfering. I would have thought that she knew he had brought it to school.

Mr Bourne   Don't worry about it. It's as I said, we can't be held responsible for everything that pupils do.

Mrs Strange   I'll see you tomorrow, then.

Mr Bourne   Yes, I suppose so. Same time, same place, same show.

He smiles bitterly.

'Bye.

Scene Twelve

Characters: Debbie, Mrs Carrington, Mr Carrington.

The next day, after school at Debbie's house. Debbie, her Mum and her Dad are in the kitchen.

Mr C.   I don't know what got into you, Debbie, I'm really disappointed in you. You, of all people.

Mrs C.   Leave her. She knows she's in the wrong and going on about it won't change anything.

Debbie   (*angrily*) I didn't do anything wrong, that's the point. You are all acting as if I've committed a major crime and I've done nothing. I wasn't involved.

Mr C.   Oh, no? Mucking around in the Art Room, selling

illegally obtained merchandise?

Mrs C. Barry!

Debbie You always think the worst of me, don't you, Dad? Okay, I was mucking around but so was everybody else. I didn't know anything about the chocolate and the money in the jar and all that. How many more times? You just carry on not believing me. I know what I did and didn't do.

Mrs C. (*sharply*) Debbie, don't be cheeky! You know your Dad's got your best interests at heart.

Debbie. (*sighing*) Oh, Mum.

Mr C. That's right, Princess, I worry about you. If you saw the half of what I see every day in the line of duty. It starts young. I don't want you mixing with hooligans and bullies.

Debbie So now you think my friends are hooligans and bullies. Karen, a bully? Don't make me laugh. You're always going on about what a suitable friend she is, about what a nice home she comes from.

She laughs sarcastically.

Make up your mind.

Mr C. (*irritated*) Less of the lip, young lady! You know very well I wasn't referring to Karen, though how she came to be involved in all this is just as much of a mystery. I thought the pair of you had more sense. Take it from me, the Smith boy and his shadow are bad news. I've had more experience of life than you, this is just the beginning for them. You mark my words, it won't be long before I'm interviewing them down the nick.

Debbie (*angrily*) I really wish I wasn't a policeman's daughter! You think you know it all, don't you? You know nothing. Daniel and Gary are my friends, they're a laugh, they are not bullies and hooligans. Who have they beaten up? Who have they bullied? Go on, tell me that! All right, so they were a bit stupid and things got out of hand, but they didn't hurt anyone.

Mr C. (*soothingly*) Princess, Princess, calm down.

Debbie (*shouting*) Don't tell me to calm down and don't call me Princess! I'm not six years old!

Mrs C. Debbie, that's enough!

Mr C. Leave her. If she can't see my point, if she can't see that having friends is one thing, going along with everything they say and do is another, that it's more important to be your own person, make your own decisions, well, I rest my case. I've had enough of this. Let her get into trouble, let her mix with the wrong sort. And by the way, Madam Princess, I'm very proud of the fact that I'm in the police force. I thought you were proud of me as well. Obviously I've got it wrong. I'm going to watch the News, call me when tea's ready.

Mrs Carrington calls after him.

Mrs C. Barry, she's only a child!

Debbie (*furiously*) I'm not a child!

Mrs C. I think you went too far, love, you've really upset him. You know he thinks the world of you.

Debbie You always take his side.

Mrs C. No, I don't. Look at it from our point of view. We get a phone call asking us to come up to the school to see the Head regarding your behaviour. That has never happened before. You're such a good girl.

Debbie But I didn't do anything, Mum.

Mrs C. I know, but it was still upsetting. Anyway, look at the way your dad took your side in the interview. He made it quite clear that we thought you had done nothing wrong. He also said that Karen should never have been trusted with those keys because it was too much responsibility for her. Just between these four walls, though, I do think you should have told a teacher about the boys setting up shop.

Debbie   But we didn't know where they had got the money to buy all those crisps and stuff. Karen didn't know that Daniel would go into the stock cupboard when she wasn't there. If she thought he might, she would have locked the cupboard before going to lunch.

Mrs C.   That's what I mean about too much responsibility. Perhaps Gary was the one who should have said something.

Debbie   Gary is Daniel's best friend, you can't grass up a friend. (*pause*) Mum, you won't let Dad stop me from seeing Karen and the others, will you?

Mrs C.   No, love. I'll have a word with him but you'll have to apologise for that outburst. You really hurt his feelings you know, especially about him being a policeman.

Mrs Carrington goes over to Debbie and gives her a hug.

Come on, give me a hand getting the tea ready.

The End

School Trip

Mollie Hemens

List of Characters

Pupils
Daniel
Gary
Mickey
Karen
Debbie
Desmond
David
Peter
Emily
Kate
Rina
Vikki
Pupils 1–4

Teachers
Ms Strange, English and Drama
Mrs Davies, Head of English
Mr Bourne, Art

Parents
Mrs Millhouse (Mrs M. – Karen's Mum)
Mrs Carrington (Mrs C. – Debbie's Mum)
Mr Carrington (Mr C. – Debbie's Dad)
Mrs De Souza (Mrs De S. – Peter's Mum)

Others
Coach Driver (Driver)
American woman (Am. Woman)
Elderly man (Eld. Man)
Elderly woman (Eld. Woman)
Alex
Steven
Ben

SCHOOL TRIP

Scene One

Characters: Debbie, Gary, Peter, Mrs Davies,
Mr Carrington, Mrs Millhouse, Mrs De Souza.

It is 5.45 a.m. Two coaches are parked outside the
school gates. Pupils and parents are gathered. The
pupils are not wearing school uniform. Mrs Davies is
answering enquiries.

Mrs Davies (*briskly*) Come along now, you were all told which
coach you were on.

Gary (*shouting*) Daniel, quick, Coach A! Leg it and grab
the back seat!

Mr C. There's that hooligan Smith. I don't want you
hanging around with him, Debbie. Do you hear?

Debbie Yes, Dad.

Mr C. Have you got your money safe?

Debbie Yes, Dad.

Mr C. What about the piece of paper with your name and
address on?

Debbie Stop fussing, Dad, I've got everything. Money,
address, food, travel pills, suntan cream, Walkman,
tapes, mascot teddy, sweater, pen, paper.

Mrs Davies (*smiling*) My goodness, Debbie, are you sure you've
got enough? That bag looks almost as big as you.

Mr C. I know. Anyone would think she was going for a
week instead of a day.

Debbie Dad!

Mrs Davies It's a long day though. Dover to Calais, twenty miles
on to the hypermarket and then on to Boulogne.

131

She takes a deep breath.

Back to Calais, the boat to Dover and home.

Mr C.   Why go to Calais? Why not go straight to Boulogne?

Mrs Davies   They've changed the rules about car ferries docking at Boulogne but the French Department still wanted to include a trip to the hypermarket.

Debbie moves from foot to foot impatiently. She sees Karen in a crowd of pupils boarding Coach A.

Debbie   Karen, save me a place near the back if you can.

Karen looks across, smiles, waves and nods. Mrs Davies and Mr Carrington are joined by Mrs Millhouse.

Mrs M.   Morning, if you can call it morning. Feels like the middle of the night to me.

Mrs Davies   Morning.

Mr C.   Morning.

Mrs M.   Rather you than me, Mrs Davies. This lot thrive on a bit of travel and excitement. Barry, I wonder if I could ask you a favour? Are you picking Debbie up tonight?

Mr C.   I'm not, I'm on late turn, but the wife is. Why?

Mrs M.   I can't get a sitter for Graham. I've got him with me in the car this morning but I don't want to keep him up late tonight to meet the coach. Not after his early start.

Mr C.   No problem. I'll tell the wife.

Mrs M.   (*relieved*) Oh, thanks. That's one less thing to worry about.

Mr C.   Sit near the front, Debbie, in case you get travel sick. Stay close to the teacher, Princess.

Debbie pretends she hasn't heard and boards the coach. Peter rushes up to Coach A, closely pursued by his mother.

Mrs De S.	(*breathless*) Wait, Peter. Don't get on the coach until I've talked to you.
Peter	But I'm late already. Me and David and Desmond want good seats.
Mrs D S.	They'll have to wait for you. It's more important that you pay attention to me.
Peter	(*resigned*) Yes, Mother.
Mrs D S.	I want you to stay with your group at all times. No wandering off. Be careful on the boat. Don't go too near the rail. No being stupid. Do you hear me?
Peter	Yes.
Mrs De S.	Well ... I know you. Off you go then.

Peter runs over to Coach A. Mrs De Souza joins Mrs Millhouse.

Mrs M.	(*smiling*) They can't wait to leave.
Mrs De S.	Let's hope they don't get too excited. That's when problems occur. I wasn't at all sure that I should have allowed Peter to go on this trip.
Mrs M.	He'll be all right.
Mrs De S.	That's a matter of opinion.

Emily, Kate, Rina and Vikki board Coach A.

Mrs De S.	Look at those girls! Do their parents know they're dressed like that?
Mrs M.	Their skirts are rather short. Still, you're only young once. I recognise one of those girls, it's Rina. She used to be very friendly with Karen at one time but they seem to have drifted apart.

She looks at her watch.

Goodness, is that the time? I must be going. Don't worry, I'm sure Peter will have a marvellous time and come back safe and sound.

Mrs De S.	(*sniffing*) Let's hope so.

Scene Two

*Characters: Daniel, Gary, Mickey, Karen, Debbie,
Desmond, David, Peter, Emily, Rina, Vikki,
Pupils 1–4, Ms Strange, Mr Bourne, Coach Driver.*

*On Coach A Gary and Daniel are guarding the back
seat. David tries to sit next to them.*

Daniel   (*aggressively*) You're not sitting here!

David   Why not?

Daniel   Because these seats are taken. Reserved. So clear off.

David   I don't know who you think you are, Smith. You're full of it. Don't want to sit next to you anyway.

David moves to the front of the coach.

Daniel   Good.

Gary unwraps a packet of sandwiches.

Daniel   What's in 'em? Egg. Good. Give us one.

Karen and Debbie join them.

Karen   What a smell! Oh no, not eating already. All you think of are your stomachs. Egg sandwiches! Gary, haven't you got any sense? You've stunk the whole coach out and we haven't even left the school gates yet.

Daniel speaks with his mouth full of sandwich.

Daniel   Stop moaning and sit down. Guarding seats makes you hungry.

Daniel moves across the seat and invitingly pats the empty space beside him.

Karen   I'm not sitting next to him. You sit there, Debbie.

Debbie   Me? (*reluctantly*) All right.

Near the front of the coach.

Desmond   Peter, over here. Sit next to me.

Peter   I hope we don't have to speak French, I don't know any.

David   You won't be able to buy anything then. They don't speak English, you know.

Desmond   (*grinning*) Don't worry, he's only joking, aren't you, David?

David   We'll look after you. You can go round with us if you like.

Mickey boards the coach and makes his way noisily to the back, greeting pupils as he goes.

Mickey   Daniel, my old mate. Cheers. Thanks for saving me a seat.

Karen   What's he doing here? Great trip this is turning out to be. First egg sandwiches, now that awful Mickey Parry.

Mickey   (*offended*) Very nice, I must say. Sit somewhere else if you don't like the view.

Karen   We would, wouldn't we, Debbie?

Debbie nods.

Only all the other seats are taken.

Mickey sees Gary's sandwiches.

Mickey   What sort are they?

He takes a sandwich and pulls it apart.

Egg. Good, I'll eat it.

Mickey stuffs most of the sandwich into his mouth in one go. Meanwhile, Gary has been watching the four girls.

Gary   Cor! Take a look at them. (*admiringly*) I didn't know they looked like that. I mean, you can't tell under that school uniform, can you? Cor! Check out those legs.

Debbie	(*sharply*) Stop dribbling, Gary! Haven't you seen legs before?
Mickey	What's up with Rina? I thought she went everywhere with you two.
Debbie	That was ages ago. She started going round with Emily after the school play. All of a sudden it was Emily this and Kate that. I can't understand it. Emily's only got one topic of conversation. Boys. Boring.
Gary	She can make a topic of me any day. I'm not fussy. I'll take any of 'em.
Karen	(*calling*) Hey, you lot! Gary doesn't know which one of you he fancies the most.

Ms Strange and Mr Bourne take their seats at the front of the coach.

Ms Strange	I'm exhausted already. I must say, Norman, school trips aren't usually your style. I had no choice. I mean, I'm their form teacher but you volunteered.
Mr Bourne	Wine, dear girl, at the hypermarket, and beer and cheese and coffee.
Ms Strange	I don't know that much about wine. What's that peculiar smell? I might have known. Gary Greene has started eating already. Gary, don't you think you should wait?
Gary	I'm hungry, Miss. Anyway, if I eat all my food now, it will be less to carry around in my bag when we get off the coach.
Mr Bourne	There's a certain logic to that.

The Coach Driver boards the coach. He speaks to the teachers.

	I do hope this lot aren't going to mess up my nice clean coach.
Ms Strange	No, I've got black plastic sacks. We'll clear up as we go along.
Driver	Good. (*pause*) And sick bags. What about sick bags?

Mr Bourne	Spare me the details.
Driver	You have to think of these things, guv'nor. Let's hope it's a calm crossing. You wait and see, I know kids. They'll eat all the way across the Channel and they'll eat all the time in France and then they'll take it in turns to throw up on the way back.
Mr Bourne	(*apprehensively*) Perhaps you had better have a word with them, Catherine.
Driver	(*grinning*) Don't look old enough does she, guv?

He winks at Mr Bourne.

	Teachers didn't look like that in my day.
Ms Strange	(*irritated*) I can assure you that I know how to do my job.
Driver	Ooh, la-di-dah. I was only joking, love. Don't take it personal.
Ms Strange	Quiet, everybody.

The pupils start to settle down.

	I want everyone to have an enjoyable day and I certainly don't want to have to spend my time telling you off.
Desmond	Go on, Miss, you know you enjoy a good shout.
Ms Strange	(*smiling*) I thought I would give my vocal cords the day off today. I will be passing through the coach at various times with a black plastic sack for your litter. Absolutely no litter to be left on the coach, please. Anyone who thinks they may be sick, see me for a sick bag.

Mickey pretends to vomit loudly.

Pupils 1–4	Mickey!
Ms Strange	Keep the volume down on your Walkmans. Don't stand up when the coach is moving. Try not to eat too much, it's still early. We'll be stopping at a service station on the way to Dover. Any questions?
Daniel	Can we have the coach video on, Miss?

Driver	No.
Vikki	How about the coach radio?
Driver	No.

The pupils groan.

Vikki speaks to Rina.

Vikki	Cheerful sort, isn't he? I like your outfit. Is it new?
Rina	Thanks, I bought the T-shirt last week. Does it go with the skirt?
Emily	Definitely. My mum wanted me to wear leggings and a sweatshirt 'cos she thought I'd be cold on the boat but it'll be hot in France, won't it? Anyway, I wanted to wear my skirt.
Rina	My mum doesn't know I'm wearing this skirt. It's my older sister's.

Ms Strange speaks to the Coach Driver.

Ms Strange	We're ready to leave now.
Driver	(*saluting*) Right you are, Maddimoysell.

He sits down at the wheel, picks up the microphone and addresses the pupils.

Right, boys and gels, listen carefully. My name is Ron and I'm your coach driver and guide for the day. That means I will be pointing out stuff as we go along. Listen and you might learn something. I hope you all paid attention to your teacher's list of prosecutions that she read out.

Peter	Prosecutions?
David	He means procedures, you know, all that stuff about what to do if you feel sick.
Driver	First stop the service station in about an hour and a half's time.

Twenty minutes later. Desmond looks out of the window. He is puzzled.

Desmond	Miss, where are we?

Ms Strange	On our way to Dover, Desmond.
Desmond	This is a funny way to go. It's the short cut my dad takes when we visit my cousins, through this housing estate. It's miles out of our way.
Mr Bourne	My goodness, the boy's right, Catherine. Where are we?

The coach slows down and comes to a halt outside a row of houses. The Coach Driver gets out of his seat.

Driver	Won't be a tick. Forgot my passport.
Mr Bourne	I do believe this is Ron's house. Well, well, well.

Mickey calls from the back of the coach.

Mickey	This is a funny service station.
Emily	What's going on, Miss?
Ms Strange	We've stopped at the coach driver's house. He's forgotten his passport.
Mickey	(*shouting*) Oi, Ron, thiry-eight cups of tea, three without sugar!

The pupils burst out laughing and became generally restless.

Ms Strange	Settle down, everyone. Look, here he comes now.

The Coach Driver returns, slightly out of breath.

Driver	That would never do. We'd have all been stuck at Dover. They wouldn't let me on the boat without my passport. Sorry about that.

Scene Three

Characters: Desmond, David, Peter, Ms Strange, Mrs Davies.

On the ferry to Calais. Ms Strange and Mrs Davies are sitting out on deck.

Mrs Davies   I had a moment's panic when we noticed your coach wasn't behind us.

Ms Strange   Yes, the coach driver made a slight detour to his house, he'd forgotten his passport. I can't say that I've really taken to him.

Desmond, David and Peter approach. Mrs Davies smiles brightly.

Mrs Davies   Hello, you three. Have you been exploring the boat?

Desmond   It's really cool, Miss. I mean, it's massive. There's so much to see.

David   Yes, we got lost and there's loads of kids from other schools, so it's quite crowded.

Peter   We tried to get a McDonald's.

Ms Strange   (*interrupting*) McDonald's, Peter? Surely not. You're getting muddled.

Peter   No, Miss. Honest, Miss. There's a big McDonald's down where all the cafés are.

Mrs Davies   Where these children find the room to put all this food is beyond me. They haven't stopped eating since we left the school gates.

Desmond   Are you going to be sitting here long, Miss?

Ms Strange   I have no immediate plans to leave the ship, Desmond.

Desmond   Can we leave our bags with you then? They're really heavy to cart about.

Ms Strange   I should have seen that one coming. All right, only fifteen minutes.

Peter   Yes, Miss. Thanks, Miss. Let's go to the shop, I want to buy a postcard of the boat.

The boys wander off.

Mrs Davies   I'll go on walkabout. You'll be all right here at base camp will you, Catherine?

Ms Strange   As long as it doesn't get too cold. Where are the others?

Mrs Davies   I think most have gone for a coffee in the lounge. Norman is patrolling the Duty Free shop, pricing the whisky. I'll see you later then.

Scene Four

Characters: Emily, Rina, Vikki.

The Ladies' toilets, C Deck. Emily, Rina and Vikki are crowded around the mirror putting on make-up.

Emily   Did you see those boys on the coach parked behind us on the car deck? Wicked! One of them's name is Alex. He's sixteen and I really fancy him.

Vikki   How do you know his name is Alex and he's sixteen?

Emily   He told me, stupid, when we were chatting on our way upstairs from the car deck.

Vikki   You don't waste much time.

Emily   So! Come with me to try and find him. He said they were going to the bar.

Rina   (*shocked*) You won't be able to go in there. You're not old enough.

Emily   Of course you can. You can go into all the public rooms on this boat.

Scene Five

Characters: Daniel, Gary, Mickey, Karen, Debbie.

Karen and Debbie in C deck lounge. Debbie is upset.

Karen Where did you last see it?

Debbie In the Ladies. It's got all my money in it. What am I going to do?

Daniel, Gary and Mickey join the girls.

Daniel What's up with Debs?

Karen She's left her jacket with all her money in it in the Ladies and now it's gone.

Mickey Idiot.

Karen Full of sympathy, aren't we?

Gary Who else was there?

Debbie Rina and her mates.

Daniel Nobody else in there?

Debbie No. Wait a minute, there was an American woman as well.

Gary What did she look like? What was she wearing?

Debbie She had blonde dyed hair, a blue sweater and one of those long floaty skirts.

Gary Let's find her. She can't have gone far, can she? There's nowhere to go, except the sea.

Mickey We've got to find the American woman before we get to France.

Debbie We don't know that she's got the jacket.

Daniel No, but it's a start. You girls go left, we'll go right and we'll meet you back here.

Scene Six

Characters: Ms Strange, Mrs Davies.

On deck Ms Strange is guarding the bags. Mrs Davies joins her.

Mrs Davies   Still here?

Ms Strange   Mmm. I'm rather annoyed with those three. I wouldn't mind a cup of coffee.

Mrs Davies   You go off then. I'll sit here for a bit, it's a good spot to pupil-watch.

Ms Strange   Did you see Vikki and friends earlier? I'm a bit concerned. They've all got really short skirts on, and I'm sure they're wearing make-up.

Mrs Davies   I'll look out for them, not that there's a lot we can do about their appearance. It is a no-uniform trip.

Ms Strange   What about the make-up?

Mrs Davies   We can't really stop them. I'll have a quiet word with them if I think it's completely outrageous.

Ms Strange   Rina is with them and you know how strict her family are.

Mrs Davies   Yes, but this business over her brother has really upset her. It can't be much fun living in that household at the moment. Do you know when he will be released?

Ms Strange   No, she hasn't spoken to me about it recently. It does seem rather unfair for him to have been taken into Youth Custody.

Mrs Davies   Well, we can't really be sure of what actually happened. We only have Rina's version of events.

Ms Strange   I don't think that she would lie over something as serious as this.

Mrs Davies   Have you seen Gary?

Ms Strange   Not to speak to. I saw him, Daniel and Mickey rush past very purposefully.

Mrs Davies They are playing detective and that can only mean trouble. It seems that Debbie Carrington has lost her jacket with all her money in it and they are trying to track down the last person who saw it.

Ms Strange Oh, dear. I mean, for the people they are trying to find as well as Debbie. How much money was in it?

Mrs Davies About £20, I think, but she's only got herself to blame. I've lost count of the number of times I've told them to look after their possessions.

Ms Strange I know, although you can't help feeling sorry for her. It's easily done.

Scene Seven

Characters: Daniel, Gary, Mickey, Desmond, David, Peter, Mr Bourne, American Woman, Elderly Man, Elderly Woman.

In the crowded Duty Free shop, Mr Bourne is browsing in the whisky section. David, Peter and Desmond enter the shop.

Desmond There's Bourney. Told you he'd be in here. Let's go and annoy him.

The boys approach Mr Bourne.

Desmond Hello, Sir. Seen anything nice to buy?

Mr Bourne looks up.

Mr Bourne Oh, it's you three.

David Haven't you seen any of the rest of the boat, Sir?

Peter It's massive, Sir, there's even a McDonald's. We …

Mr Bourne	(*interrupting*) Yes, yes, I'm sure you're right. Haven't you got anywhere else to go? There's nothing in here for you to buy. Run along, can't you see I'm busy?
Desmond	I thought I'd get my Mum some chocolates but they might melt. Perhaps I should buy them on the way back. What do you think, Sir?
Mr Bourne	(*irritated*) What?
Desmond	Chocolates, Sir. Which sort ...?

Mickey, Daniel and Gary enter the shop. They are wearing sunglasses and looking furtive.

Mickey	(*purposefully*) Right, let's case the joint.
Daniel	Oh, no, there's Bourney.
Gary	Where?
Daniel	(*pointing*) Over there, by the booze.
Mickey	Quick! Drop!

Mickey and Daniel fall to the floor, roll over and assume a crouching position behind a stack of chocolate boxes. Gary remains standing.

Daniel	Get down, Gary!
Gary	I feel stupid. Why are we wearing sunglasses?
Daniel	So we don't get recognised.
Gary	Oh, yeah.

He drops down to a crouching position. Mickey peers round the chocolate boxes.

Mickey	Over there.
Gary	Where?
Mickey	A couple of aisles away from Bourney. It's the American woman.

Gary and Daniel peer round the chocolate boxes.

Daniel	And she's got Debbie's jacket.
Gary	What do we do now?

Mickey   I need to get a closer look. You two stay here and cover me till I give the signal.

Mickey stands up, adjusts his sunglasses, relaxes his shoulders, smooths back his hair and strolls over towards the American woman. A little way before he reaches her, he drops to a crouching position, pauses and then slowly crawls forward, through the crowd of shoppers, trying to avoid their legs. An elderly couple notice Mickey. The Elderly Man nudges his wife.

Eld. Man   Dorothy, what do you think that boy is up to? It seems highly suspect to me.

Eld. Woman   Who, dear?

Eld. Man   That boy crawling around on the floor wearing sunglasses.

Eld. Woman   Oh, yes.

The elderly couple watch Mickey as he crawls through the shoppers.

Eld. Man   I think he's trying to steal from people's shopping bags. Look, he's positioned himself right next to that young woman's bag. I'm going to tackle him.

Eld. Woman   (*worried*) Do you think you ought to, dear? He might be dangerous.

Eld. Man   I think someone should ask him just what he thinks he's up to. No one else seems to have noticed.

Eld. Woman   Perhaps we should find someone in authority.

Eld. Man   It will be too late by then. He will have stolen from everyone in sight and got away with the lot. You stay here. I'll go and have a sharp word with him.

Eld. Woman   Do be careful, dear.

The American Woman is looking at bottles of sherry. Meanwhile, David is trying to attract Mr Bourne's attention. Mr Bourne looks across just in time to see the American Woman trip over Mickey.

Am. Woman	Oh, my!

She looks down at Mickey.

	What do you think you are doing?
Mr Bourne	(*appalled*) Good grief, this is all I need!

Mr Bourne disappears behind the wine aisles. Mickey gets to his feet. Daniel and Gary rush up.

Daniel	That's my friend Debbie's jacket and she wants it back.
Am. Woman	Excuse me?
Gary	That jacket you are holding. It belongs to our friend.

The American Woman examines the jacket.

Am. Woman	Yes, I found it in the Rest-Room. I'm going to hand it in to the Purser's Office just as soon as I'm done here.
Mickey	(*sarcastically*) I'm sure. You can hand it to us instead and save yourself the bother.
Am. Woman	(*outraged*) Really!

Meanwhile, David is trying to attract Mr Bourne's attention again.

David	(*urgently*) Sir!
Mr Bourne	What now, boy?
David	They're shouting at each other.
Peter	Aren't you going to do something, Sir?
Desmond	I think you should, Sir.
Mr Bourne	(*sighing*) I suppose I must.

Mr Bourne goes over to the American Woman. Desmond, David and Peter follow.

Mr Bourne	Excuse me, Madam, is there a problem? These pupils are in my charge.
Am. Woman	Problem? Oh, no problem. Unless you call looking up my skirt a problem.
Mickey	I never …

Mr Bourne	Shut up, boy, you've caused enough trouble. When I want your opinion I will ask for it. Now, perhaps someone can explain.

Elderly Man joins them.

Eld. Man	Excuse me for interrupting but I couldn't help overhearing your conversation and I think I can supply you with an explanation.

Mickey stares at the Elderly Man in surprise.

Eld. Man	It's no good looking as if you don't know what's going on, boy. Don't come playing the innocent with me. My wife and I have been watching you for some time. You were attempting to steal from shopping bags.
Mickey	I never ...
Mr Bourne	Stop interrupting, Parry. I won't tell you again. It seems to me that you are in quite a lot of bother. You are accused of stealing and looking up ladies' skirts. What do you have to say for yourself?
Eld. Man	That's the ticket, take a firm line with him. Young people today can't be trusted at all. Now, in my day ...
Mr Bourne	Yes, yes. If you will allow me to question the boy, I'm his teacher.
Gary	It's not what you think, Sir. Debbie lost her jacket with all her money in it. And that lady has got it.
Am. Woman	I was trying to explain to them. I found it in the Rest-Room. I was on my way to hand it in and they all but accused me of stealing it.
Daniel	We never, Sir. We were just trying to find Debbie's jacket. We didn't know she was going to hand it in. We just saw her with it.
Mr Bourne	I should have known that you and Greene would be involved, Smith. Am I supposed to believe everything you tell me, with your track record? Don't make me laugh.

The American Woman interrupts impatiently.

Am. Woman I don't know what this conversation is about and I don't care. You can have the jacket.

She throws the jacket to Mickey, who catches it.

If these are examples of British schoolchildren they are not good ambassadors for their country. I've had enough of this nonsense.

Mr Bourne Wait, Madam. I think that at the very least an apology is called for.

Mickey Yes, Sir. Sorry, Sir.

Mr Bourne Not me, you fool, her.

Mickey turns to the American Woman.

Mickey Sorry.

Am. Woman I'm sure glad I'm not your teacher. Are you always this dumb?

Gary We really are sorry. We just didn't think.

She turns to Mr Bourne.

Am. Woman I'll say. I'd just as soon drop the whole thing.

Mr Bourne (*relieved*) Thank you. I can only apologise once again for their appalling behaviour. I can assure you that the matter will be taken up by my superiors when we return to school. Perhaps you could give me your address so that we can send you an official letter of apology.

Am. Woman That won't be necessary. I don't need all this hassle.

The American Woman leaves the shop. Mr Bourne speaks to the Elderly Man.

Mr Bourne I appreciate your concern. I only wish that more members of the public were as observant as you. However, it does seem as if the matter has been successfully resolved. Thank you.

Eld. Man Think nothing of it, old chap. Glad to have been of use.

Mr Bourne turns to Mickey, Daniel and Gary.

Mr Bourne   I will deal with you three later. Make sure that you give Debbie her jacket back.

Mr Bourne leaves the shop. The Elderly Man rejoins his wife.

Eld. Woman   What happened, dear? Is everything all right?

Eld. Man   Yes, the teacher chappie sorted it all out. Seems that we got it wrong. The boy wasn't stealing, he was looking up women's skirts. Some sort of pervert if you ask me.

Eld. Woman   Oh, my goodness!

Scene Eight

Characters: Daniel, Gary, Mickey, Karen, Debbie, Desmond, David, Peter, Emily, Kate, Rina, Vikki, Ms Strange, Mr Bourne, Coach Driver.

Coach A. On the way to the hypermarket.

At the back of the coach.

Debbie   I can't believe I got my jacket back with all my money in it.

Karen   You were lucky, it just proves that there are some honest people about.

Daniel   If it hadn't been for us you wouldn't have got it back.

Gary   Lucky for you that Bourney couldn't be bothered.

Mickey   Yeah, he only asked that woman for her address. He's too old to be interested in women.

Karen   Sometimes I wonder where you keep your brain.

Daniel said that Mr Bourne wanted her address so that the school could send her a letter of apology.

Mickey   Excuses, excuses.

Karen   You really are stupid, Mickey.

Mickey   Well, we can't be greedy can we? You've got the brains and I've got the looks.

Gary tries to stand up and beat his chest.

Gary   What about me? I've got both.

There is a general scramble and laughter as the others try to push Gary back into his seat.

In the middle of the coach.

Emily   (*sighing*) He's lovely. I think I'm in love.

Vikki   You're mad, you're never going to see him again.

Emily   Yes, I am. So it shows you how much you know. We're getting the same boat back and you never know, I might bump into him in Boulogne.

Kate   I liked his friend, Steven, but I think he was a bit shy.

Vikki   Let's face it, girl, he just didn't fancy you.

Rina   That's a bit cruel, Vikki. Just because you didn't meet anybody.

Vikki   What about you? You were struck dumb, you were no fun at all.

Rina   I didn't come on this trip to find a boyfriend.

Kate   Stop arguing. We've got to think of a way to help Emily and Alex get together.

Near the front of the coach.

Desmond   I think Bourney spent the whole crossing in Duty Free. Well, most of it anyway.

David   He got really shirty with us, didn't he, when we tried saying hello?

Desmond   What about Mickey Parry? Fancy crawling around on all fours wearing sunglasses.

Peter   What do you think will happen to them when they get back to school?

David   Don't know.

At the front of the coach.

Mr Bourne   I was very embarrassed, I can tell you. Crawling around on all fours, wearing sunglasses. If I could have pretended that I didn't know him, I would have.

Ms Strange   What did the American woman say?

Mr Bourne   Not a lot. She thought that Parry was trying to look up her skirt. The Smith boy accused her of stealing Debbie's coat. No excuse me, or please, or thank you. Then to cap it all, some old fellow decides to be a responsible citizen.

Ms Strange   Sounds awful. What action did you take?

Mr Bourne   I made the pupils apologise, of course. I even asked the woman for her address so that the school could send an official letter of apology but she wasn't interested.

The Coach Driver speaks through the microphone.

Driver   Testing, testing. Can you hear me at the back?

Karen   Yes.

Mickey   No.

Driver   Right, boys and gels. If you look out the window on the left hand side of the coach, you will see a big expedition all about the Channel Tunnel. It is well worth a visit if you come back another day.

Peter   What's he on about?

David   He means exhibition.

Driver   We are nearly at the hypermarket. When we get there, do as your teacher tells you. Stick together and don't go nicking nothing.

Ms Strange interrupts loudly.

Ms Strange   Thank you, Ron. I can take over from here. If I could just borrow the microphone?

She speaks privately to Mr Bourne.

I don't need him to tell me how to do my job.

Driver   (*offended*) I heard that. Only trying to help, suit yourself.

Ms Strange   As you leave the coach, I will be handing out a worksheet for you to complete. Take it seriously and try your best. It will go towards your end of term assessment.

Daniel   I knew there'd be a catch just when I was starting to enjoy myself.

Scene Nine

Characters: Daniel, Gary, Mickey, Karen, Debbie, Desmond, David, Peter, Emily, Kate, Rina, Vikki, Pupils 1–4, Mrs Davies, Coach Driver.

At the hypermarket. David, Peter and Desmond are standing by an empty shopping trolley.

David   You remember what you have to do?

Peter   I find Mrs Davies and keep her occupied by asking questions about the worksheet.

Peter   If you ask me, it's a daft idea. What about the other teachers? They're bound to notice.

Desmond   No, they won't. Most of them head for the booze aisles, Bourney leading the way.

David   I've never seen him move so fast. Did you see the size of his trolley? He had one of those massive ones

and Ms Strange was having trouble keeping up with
him.

Desmond She won't hang around the wine for long. She'll start
patrolling, just like Mrs Davies. We've got to be
quick, before they've got their booze and they've
moved on.

Peter Why do I have to keep Mrs Davies occupied? Why
not one of you?

David Because you don't understand anything on that
worksheet anyway, so you won't have to pretend to
ask for help.

Peter It's not fair.

Desmond Stop moaning. We're splitting the profits aren't we?
Let's go.

In the cheese section.

Emily *Fromage.* That's cheese. What do we have to do?

Rina List as many cheeses as we can and say where they
come from.

Kate Boring!

Emily You're telling me, there's not a decent looking bloke
in sight.

Vikki That's all you think about all the time.

Emily Absolutely!

In the sweets aisle.

Mickey That cheese part was disgusting. How can anybody
eat stuff that smells like that?

Karen No worse than Gary's egg sandwiches.

Debbie I'm going to buy some cheese for my Dad.

Mickey Don't sit next to me on the way back.

Debbie Chance would be a fine thing.

In the car park, by the coach.

Driver (*admiringly*) Very enterprising, lads. How much
have you bought?

Desmond   Nine crates.

David   It's really hot today. All we have to do is wait for them to get back to the coaches, uncap a bottle or two and start collecting the money.

Peter rushes up, out of breath.

Peter   I've finished all of the worksheet. Well, Mrs Davies did, so we should get a really high mark. Have you sold many bottles?

Desmond   No, we're waiting for them to come back to the coaches.

David   I hope this works.

Desmond   It will, think positive. Anyway, we can always drink it ourselves.

David   I don't even like Coke.

Desmond   All the more for me then.

Daniel, Mickey and Gary join them.

Gary   Cor! Coca-Cola. Give us one.

Desmond   Certainly. That will be thirty pence please.

Gary   What?

David   Thirty pence a bottle.

Mickey   But they're only little bottles.

Desmond   Buy two then.

Daniel   Go on, my treat. Will you take French money?

David   Notes only, no coins.

Mickey   We shouldn't have to buy it from this lot.

Daniel   I'm buying, not you. Stay thirsty for all I care.

Desmond takes the money, opens three bottles and hands them over. More pupils gradually join them and trade is brisk.

Peter   Look out! Here comes Mrs Davies.

Mrs Davies approaches.

Mrs Davies   So this is your game. Now I know why you were so

keen on my company, Peter. Right, get this lot put
away into the coach luggage hold.

Pupil 1	Oh, Miss!
Pupil 2	Go on.
Pupil 3	Let's buy some.
Pupil 4	We're thirsty.
Driver	Go on, Miss, it won't hurt. I think it's a good idea myself.
Mrs Davies	(*firmly*) When I want your opinion, Ron, I'll ask for it. In the meantime, I'm in charge of their conduct and I would be grateful if you could load all this Coca-Cola into the baggage hold.

Mrs Davies walks away quickly.

Driver	Right dragon ain't she, lads? Spoils all the fun. Ah well, come on, let's get loaded up. Next stop Boulogne.

Scene Ten

*Characters: Daniel, Gary, Mickey, Karen, Debbie,
Desmond, David, Peter, Ms Strange.*

*The pedestrian-only tourist shopping area,
Boulogne. Ms Strange is briefing her group of pupils.*

Ms Strange	Two girls and six boys, I don't know how I managed it. And one of those boys is you, Mickey. Oh well, I suppose you have to be in somebody's group.
Mickey	(*offended*) Thanks a lot.
Ms Strange	See if you can keep him out of mischief, girls.
Karen	(*grinning*) We'll try. We'll make him speak French.

Mickey	No chance.
Ms Strange	This is a very small shopping precinct. I will place myself strategically at this café table.

She points to an adjacent table.

I can see from one end of the street to the other, so you can have forty-five minutes on your own. Don't go beyond that café at the top of the street. Can you see it?

The pupils peer in the direction she is pointing.

The one with the windmill on its sign, the Moulin Rouge.

Debbie	Yes, Miss.
Ms Strange	And don't go beyond this café here. I'll be sitting at this table if you need me.
Daniel	(*muttering*) Big deal, there's only half a dozen shops between here and that windmill place.
Ms Strange	Are you complaining, Daniel?
Gary	(*quickly*) No, he isn't.
Ms Strange	Good, because if he is he can stay with me.
Mickey	We'll be good, Miss, promise. You sit here and have a nice cup of tea. I'll keep them in order.

The others laugh.

Ms Strange	Very reassuring, Mickey, I must say.

Daniel, Gary, Mickey, Karen and Debbie walk over to a tourist shop.

Ms Strange	What about you three? I'll buy you a drink if you can order it in French.
Desmond	You're on. Une verre du vin rouge, s'il vous plait.
Ms Strange	(*smiling*) Very impressive, but I meant a soft drink.
David	We've got a coach full of those, Miss.
Peter	(*worried*) I'm not very good at speaking French.
Ms Strange	(*relenting*) All right, come on, it will be my treat, Desmond can order.

Scene Eleven

Characters: Karen, Debbie, Emily, Kate, Rina, Vikki, Alex, Steven, Ben.

Emily, Kate, Rina and Vikki are sitting at a café table. Rina is writing a postcard.

Kate   Who's the card to, Rina?

Rina   No one you know, just a friend. I send him a postcard whenever I visit anywhere new.

Vikki Secret boyfriend. Tell us. Name, age, is he good looking, where did you meet him?

Rina   Why do relationships with boys have to be romantic? Why can't it just be friends?

Emily Because being just good friends is boring.

Rina   (*irritated*) I don't think so. We haven't all got one-track minds.

Emily interrupts excitedly.

Emily Over there! Look! No, don't look! Turn your head slowly and pretend to be looking somewhere else.

Rina, Kate and Vikki turn simultaneously. A group of boys are lounging outside the shop opposite the cafe. They are watching the girls and laughing amongst themselves.

Emily I didn't mean all look at once. You're so embarrassing.

Vikki I think it's them. Alex has got short blonde hair, hasn't he?

Kate   Steven is with them.

Emily They're coming over. Act cool.

Alex   Good afternoon, girls. Mind if we join you?

Kate and Vikki giggle. Emily glares at them.

Emily	It's a free country.
	The boys sit down. There is an awkward silence. Ben speaks to Rina.
Ben	All right?
	Rina turns away.
Rina	Fine, thanks.
Ben	Friendly, isn't she?
Emily	Take no notice, she's shy.
Steven	What do you think of Boulogne?
Kate	Not a lot. They've only let us off our leads for half an hour.
Alex	What year are you in?
Emily	(*quickly*) Year Nine.
Alex	Understandable, then. They worry about you little ones. Wait till you're in Year Ten, like us.
Vikki	Cheek!
Ben	Yeah, it gets you everywhere.
	He takes out a pack of cigarettes.
	Smoke, anyone?
Steven	Thanks.
Alex	Don't mind if I do.
Emily	Okay.
	Ben holds out the pack.
Ben	Girls?
Vikki	Sure you don't mind? You haven't got many left.
Kate	What if a teacher sees us?
Emily	Grow up for a while.
	Vikki and Kate each take a cigarette. Alex gets out a lighter and they all light their cigarettes.
Emily	Here, Rina, take a drag of mine.

Rina   I don't smoke.

Emily   You've never tried. Go on, take a drag.

Emily passes the cigarette to Rina, who hesitates then takes it.

Nice and slow, don't swallow it.

Rina draws on the cigarette and chokes slightly. They all laugh. Karen and Debbie pass by their table.

Debbie   Hi, Rina, I didn't know you smoked.

Rina   You learn something new every day, don't you?

Debbie   (*offended*) I only asked, there's no need to bite my head off. You'd better make sure Ms Strange doesn't catch you. She's not far away.

Emily   (*imitating*) '*She's not far away.*' So? She won't see us, will she?

Kate   Haven't you two got somewhere else to go? Push off.

Karen   (*quietly*) I think Debbie was talking to her friend Rina.

Debbie   Leave it, Karen, if that's the sort of company she keeps, good luck to her. Let's go.

Debbie and Karen move off.

Vikki   'Bye 'bye.

Rina looks uncomfortable.

Emily   Forget it, Rina. They're just a couple of kids.

Steven   They don't look very old.

Emily   They're just stupid Year Seven kids.

Rina   But I used to be really good friends with them.

Alex   What? With Year Sevens?

Rina   Well …

Emily   (*interrupting*) Haven't we got anything better to do than discuss those two?

Ben   Yeah, all this girl talk is boring. Where are you lot from? Have you got boyfriends?

Emily leans across to Alex.

Emily   I'm open to offers from the right person.

Vikki   Emily!

Alex   Flattery will get you everywhere. Fancy a quiet stroll?

Emily   Okay.

Emily and Alex stand up.

See you later, girls.

Emily and Alex stroll off.

Steven   They didn't waste much time. Good idea, though. Fancy a stroll, Vikki?

Vikki hesitates and glances across at Kate.

No, thanks, I quite like sitting here.

Ben   Now, where were we? Where did you say you were from?

Scene Twelve

Characters: Emily, Kate, Rina, Vikki, Desmond, David, Peter, Mrs Davies, Coach Driver.

One and a half hours later. The coach park, Boulogne.

David   Thanks, Ron.

Driver   That's all right, mate. I'm all for enterprise. Grab hold of this crate of Coke.

Desmond	Peter, you take the money and I'll open the bottles. David, keep an eye out for teachers.

A group of pupils gather round and start to buy Coca-Cola.

Vikki	I'll have two, please. Sure you don't want one, Kate?
Kate	(*sulkily*) Sure.

She boards the coach.

Vikki	(*shrugging*) Suit yourself.

Desmond uncaps two bottles and hands them to Vikki and Rina.

Rina	I wonder where Emily has got to, it's getting ever so late.
Vikki	She's a big girl, she can look after herself.
Rina	That Steven really fancied you.
Vikki	Kate fancied him. I couldn't do that to a mate, you know, steal her bloke.
Rina	But he wasn't her bloke.
Vikki	You know what I mean. Where's Emily? I wish she'd get a move on.

Rina and Vikki board the coach.

Peter	That will be thirty pence. Here, Desmond, open this bottle for me.
Desmond	You open it, Pete. I've got to get another crate from the coach.

Peter starts to open the bottle. He misses the cap and gashes the palm of his hand badly.

Peter	(*urgently*) Aagh, Help, I'm bleeding! Desmond, quick, help me!
Desmond	You idiot! Drop the bottle. Why were you holding it so close to the top?
David	That's a lot of blood. Hold your hand up. Mrs Davies is over there. Miss, quick!

Mrs Davies rushes up. She clears a path through the pupils.

Mrs Davies What's happened? Let me through.

She sees Peter holding up this blood-soaked hand.

Oh, my goodness! All pupils on to the coach immediately. Ron, get the First Aid kit, please.

Peter It hurts.

Mrs Davies Stop fussing, Peter.

The Coach Driver gives Mrs Davies the First Aid Kit.

Driver Can I do anything to help?

Mrs Davies (*frostily*) I think you have done enough for one day.

Driver Suit yourself, but it looks to me like he's tried to severe his hand off.

Mrs Davies Sever, Ron, the word is sever. I would like to get this boy's hand attended to and be on our way to Calais. All I need is for us to miss the ferry, we're already running late.

Emily rushes up, out of breath.

Mrs Davies Emily, just the person. Someone I can rely on. Run and find one of the other teachers and say that there has been an accident.

Emily looks surprised. She doesn't move.

Mrs Davies Hurry up, girl, don't stand there gaping!

Emily (*grinning*) Yes, Mrs Davies.

Scene Thirteen

Characters: Daniel, Gary, Mickey, Karen, Debbie, Desmond, David, Peter, Emily, Kate, Rina, Vikki, Ms Strange, Mr Bourne, Coach Driver.

Several hours later, in Coach A on the car deck of the ferry. At the front of the coach.

Mr Bourne I'm exhausted. Still, quite a good day. It was kind of Ron to help me load all my shopping into the luggage hold. (*pause*) I feel sorry for Ann having to mop up the De Souza boy.

Ms Strange It was rather a lot of blood. Fortunately it looked worse than it really was.

Mr Bourne Another couple of hours and we'll be home. I've saved a fortune buying in bulk.

Ms Strange I wish we were off this ferry and on the road. They might calm down a bit once we're moving.

She stands up and addresses the pupils in a loud voice.

Would you calm down and sit down. All those people who are standing up should go back to their seats now.

In the middle of the coach.

Emily (*sighing*) Oh, Alex. He lives in St Albans. I don't know when I'll see him again.

Kate It'll be what you might call a distance romance.

Emily I've written his phone number on the back of my hand.

She holds out her hand.

See.

Vikki And she'll never wash again.

Kate	You were lucky, you nearly missed the coach at Boulogne.
Emily	Kind of Peter to create a diversion. I didn't know what was going on at first. When Mrs Davies called me over, I thought I was in for a right telling-off.

She sighs.

Oh, Alex.

Rina	How am I going to get all this make-up off? (*pause*) Oh, no!
Kate	What?
Rina	I forgot. My Dad doesn't know I'm wearing this skirt. He'll go mad. What shall I do?
Vikki	Say that you spilt ice-cream down yours and you borrowed a spare one of mine.
Rina	He'll want to know where my own skirt is.
Vikki	Tell him I've taken it home to wash.
Rina	It'll never work.
Emily	Tell him the truth then and get your sister into trouble as well.
Rina	I don't care anyway. What can he do, ground me, yell at me? Big deal.
Emily	Now you're talking. Anyway, Alex has got my phone number on his hand. Do you think I should wait for him to phone me or should I phone him first?
Kate	You weren't shy in Boulogne so phone him. And as for the ferry, you were lucky no teachers spotted you.
Emily	We were only having a cuddle, that's all. What's wrong with that? You're just jealous that you didn't get off with Steven.
Kate	I couldn't care less about Steven, it's Vikki who fancied him anyway.
Vikki	(*outraged*) I didn't!
Rina	Let's just drop it, shall we? We've got to complete

the worksheet, so let's do it now.

Near the front of the coach.

Peter Ouch! Don't knock my hand. It hurts.

David Good. Thanks to you, we've got an appointment with the Head tomorrow.

Desmond It's not fair. I bet you anything that Mickey and that lot get away with all that business in the Duty Free shop.

David That's because Bourney caught them and Mrs Davies caught us.

Desmond It's the luck of the draw, you win some, you lose some.

Peter It's not the Head I'm worried about, it's my Mum. You know what she's like.

David How much have we got left?

Desmond Four crates.

Peter No, we haven't, I sold a crate to Daniel Smith in exchange for the worksheet answers.

Desmond Nice one, Pete. That's a crate each left over. Not a bad day's work.

David You know I don't like Coke.

Desmond Tough. Feed your share to the cat.

At the back of the coach.

Debbie Get Rina. Who does she think she is?

Karen She's okay. She didn't mean to put you down.

Debbie It's those new mates of hers. Did you see Emily with that boy in the lounge on the ferry? Talk about flaunting yourself! I don't know why Rina goes round with them. Talk about trying to act hard!

Karen She's okay. She's just got a few problems at the moment.

Debbie How do you know?

Karen Remember that weekend when you had to go to

your uncle's party and Rina stayed over at my house?

Debbie nods.

Well, she told me some stuff about herself and her family.

Pause.

Debbie	Well?
Karen	Well, what?
Debbie	What sort of stuff?
Karen	I can't tell you because I promised Rina I'd keep it a secret.
Debbie	(*offended*) I'm your best friend, you can tell me.
Karen	No, I can't. A promise is a promise.
Debbie	(*wheedling*) Go on, tell me. I won't tell anyone.
Karen	(*firmly*) No.
Debbie	(*angrily*) Suit yourself. Just don't expect me to tell you anything, that's all. I thought we were best mates.

Debbie turns away and looks out of the window.

Gary	What's the hold-up? It's ever so hot on this coach.
Mickey	Yeah, I feel sick.
Daniel	You lot owe me seventy-two pence each.
Karen	What for?
Daniel	'Cos that's how much it cost me to get the worksheet answers from that creep De Souza. Work it out.
Debbie	The cheese I bought has melted.
Gary	It smells horrible.
Mickey	Yeah, I feel sick.

The coach engine starts up.

Daniel	We're off.
Mickey	I'm going to be sick.

Karen	Stop messing about, Mickey.

She suddenly realises he is serious.

	Quick, somebody get a bag!
Debbie	(*shouting*) Miss, Mickey is feeling sick.
Daniel	Too late.

Mickey is sick.

At the front of the coach.

Ms Strange	Ron, I'm terribly sorry but one of the pupils has been sick.
Driver	(*agitated*) Don't bother me now, dear.
Ms Strange	But, Ron …
Driver	I'm having a bit of trouble with me coach. Later, dear, later.
Mr Bourne	I knew it was too good to last.
Desmond	What's going on, Miss? The coach is making funny noises.
Ms Strange	Everyone stay calm and that will help Ron. Sit down and remain seated.
Gary	There's sick all over my seat, Miss.
Mickey	I don't feel very well.
Daniel	Ugh, this coach really stinks, what with his sick and her cheese.

Scene Fourteen

*Characters: Karen, Desmond, David, Peter, Emily,
Kate, Rina, Vikki, Ms Strange, Mr Bourne.*

*On the beach in Dover. Ms Strange and Mr Bourne
are sitting on the pebbles. They are surrounded by
pupils' belongings.*

Mr Bourne   Ron says it's a major engine problem, so goodness
knows how long we'll be. He's been in touch with
his company and they are sending out a
replacement coach.

Ms Strange   At least it isn't raining and we can wait on the
beach.

*She points to a group of pupils who are throwing
pebbles into the sea.*

They seem to be enjoying themselves. What time do
you think the other coach will be here?

Mr Bourne   I would say about another hour.

Desmond, David and Peter join them.

Desmond   I'm really tired.

He flops down on to the pebbles.

How much longer will it be?

Ms Strange   About an hour.

David   An hour? I'll miss the football on the telly.

Ms Strange   My heart's breaking for you.

Peter   My hand's hurting.

Mr Bourne   Don't expect any sympathy from me, boy. I've just
about had enough of all of you for one day. It's the
last school trip I go on.

Ms Strange   You'll be all right, Peter. Why don't you three go and
see what the others are up to?

David   They're throwing pebbles into the sea. We tried to join in but they told us to clear off.

Ms Strange   Stay here with us then. We can play a word game. Mr Bourne, would you like to play a game with us?

Mr Bourne   No, thank you, I think I will go and keep Ron company.

Mr Bourne gets up and walks to the car park. Emily, Kate, Rina and Vikki are sitting on another part of the beach. Karen joins them.

Emily   Where's your friend?

Karen   Who? Oh, you mean Debbie. She's over there somewhere.

Karen points vaguely in the direction of a group of girls who are further along the beach.

Vikki   Had an argument, have we?

Karen   No, why do you think that?

Vikki   I thought you two couldn't be separated, like Siamese twins.

Rina   Leave her, Vikki. Do you want a sandwich, Karen? I've got some left.

Karen   (*laughing*) Yes, please, as long as they're not lettuce.

Emily   What's so funny?

Karen   It's the lettuce joke, haven't you heard it? Gary thinks that too much lettuce makes you pregnant. We wind him up about it.

Kate   Do you want children, Karen?

Karen   I've got enough problems now, without thinking about the future.

Emily   I can't wait to be older. I'll be able to see the films I want to see and go into pubs and arrange my love life.

Vikki   You don't seem to have any difficulty at the moment.

Kate	At least blokes fancy you.
Emily	Yeah, but how am I going to meet up with Alex again? He's lovely, I miss him already.
Rina	Here we go again. Alex, Alex, Alex. It's getting very boring.
Karen	Who's Alex?
Rina	Don't ask her that, you won't be able to shut her up.
Emily	(*offended*) He's a boy I met on the ferry going to Calais.
Kate	Anyway, Karen, you didn't answer my question. Do you want children?
Karen	Maybe some time in the future, many years from now.
Vikki	I'm never going to get married. I'm going to have my own house, car, and business.
Kate	Won't you be lonely?
Vikki	No way. I'll be too busy thinking how to spend all my money from my important job.
Rina	I want a good education so that I can earn enough to leave home and never go back.
Kate	(*shocked*) I'm never going to leave my Mum. I want a nice house and a nice husband and two kids. A boy first, then a girl.
Vikki	Excuse me while I throw up.
Karen	Each to their own. What about you, Emily?
Emily	I want to know how I can visit Alex without my Mum finding out.
Rina	Emily! Let's get her, quick!

Peter runs up to the girls.

Peter	Message from Ms Strange. The other coach is here so we've got to go to the car park.
Karen	About time too.

Scene Fifteen

Characters: Daniel, Mickey, Karen, Debbie,
Desmond, David, Peter, Kate, Rina, Ms Strange,
Mrs Davies, Mr Bourne, Coach Driver,
Mrs Carrington, Mrs De Souza.

Late that night outside the school, a group of
parents and teachers are waiting for Coach A.

Mrs C.   The communication system didn't work very well.
               No one phoned me to say they would be late. I
               arrived here over two hours ago only to be told that
               the coach had broken down.

Mrs Davies I do apologise. Apparently they managed to get off the
                ferry but could go no further and the coach company
                had to send another coach to collect them.

Mrs De S.   What? I don't believe it.

Mrs C.   Why couldn't they get it mended in Dover?

Mrs De S.   (*sarcastically*) Oh, that's too easy.

Mrs Davies There wasn't a garage that carried the part.

Mrs C.   As long as everybody is all right.

Mrs De S.   I think it's very inefficient of the coach company.

Mrs Davies Breakdowns do happen. I think I should tell you,
                Mrs De Souza, that …

Mrs C.   (*interrupting*) Look, here it comes now.

Coach A slowly draws up to a halt. The pupils noisily
prepare to leave the coach. Ms Strange shouts above
the noise.

Ms Strange Make sure that you have left no rubbish behind. Also
                check for belongings.

The pupils ignore her.

Okay, that's it. I've had enough. Everybody sit down
and shut up now!

The pupils do as they are told.

That's better. I don't care if it is the middle of the night, there are some rules that must be observed.

Driver (*approvingly*) That's right, you tell 'em, Miss.

Ms Strange ignores him.

Ms Strange On your behalf, I would like to thank our coach driver for all he's done and for coping with the mechanical problems at Dover.

The pupils cheer.

Mr Bourne Hear, hear.

Ms Strange And well done, most of you, for behaving in a responsible and mature fashion.

At the back of the coach.

Daniel I wish she'd hurry up, droning on. You stink, Mickey.

Mickey (*mournfully*) I can't help it, it was Debbie's fault with that cheese.

Debbie Blame me, why don't you? It might have had something to do with all that Coke you drank. Not to mention the chips, the ice-cream and Gary's egg sandwiches.

Mickey Leave off, I don't feel well.

Karen Good.

She turns to Debbie.

Shall I meet you before school tomorrow, Debbie?

Debbie (*sulkily*) Don't know.

Karen Well, I'll be at the usual place.

In the middle of the coach.

Kate looks out of the window.

Kate There's your dad, Rina. Put my coat on, it's longer than your skirt. Tell him you're cold and maybe he won't notice in the dark.

Rina Thanks, I'll let you have it back tomorrow.

Near the front of the coach.

Peter I'm not looking forward to this. Can you two come and meet my Mum with me?

Desmond You'll be all right, I want to get home.

David You don't know his Mum as well as I do. She'll give him a right ear bashing.

The pupils disembark from the coach.

Karen 'Bye, Debbie, I'll see you tomorrow.

Debbie doesn't reply and goes to join her mother. Karen walks away slowly.

Mrs C. Hello, love, you look tired. Did you have a nice time?

Debbie It was all right but I didn't like all the time we had to spend on the coach, especially after Mickey Parry was sick.

Mrs De S. You poor things. It must have been dreadful stranded in Dover.

Debbie That was one of the best bits. We went on to the beach. It was a laugh.

Mrs C. Where's Karen?

Debbie She's gone home.

Mrs C. She can't have. I'm supposed to be collecting her. Really, Debbie!

Debbie How was I supposed to know?

Mrs C. Quick! Run and find her before she starts to walk home on her own.

Debbie Do I have to?

Mrs C. So that's the way the land lies. You two have fallen out.

Debbie We have not!

Mrs C. We're giving her a lift anyway so run after her quickly and catch her up.

Debbie reluctantly goes in search of Karen.
Ms Strange greets Mrs Davies.

Ms Strange   Am I glad to see you!

Mrs Davies   I think you coped admirably. How did you keep them occupied in Dover?

Ms Strange   We took them to the beach. A brainwave on my part, I thought. They loved it. They thought it was the best part of the trip.

She sighs.

You just can't win.

Peter greets his mother.

Mrs De S.   (*shocked*) What happened? I let you out of my sight for the day and this is how you return.

Peter   It's all right, Mother, honest, it's just a little scratch.

Mrs De S.   I'll little scratch you. How did it happen? You were fooling about as usual, I expect.

Mr Bourne joins them.

Mr Bourne   It seems worse than it is, Mrs De Souza.

Mrs De S.   It's not good enough. I want to know exactly what happened and who was in charge. And another thing, I don't expect to be spoken to so rudely by the coach driver. I only asked him for the telephone number of the coach company so that I could find out exactly what went wrong with the coach. He was extremely rude. I think he's been drinking.

Mr Bourne   I can assure you, Mrs De Souza, that I have spent most of the day with Ron and he has not touched a drop of alcohol. In fact, he has been most cheerful and helpful.

Mrs De Souza suddenly notices the wine and beer in the open luggage hold.

Mrs De S.   My goodness, who does all that belong to?

Mr Bourne   (*quickly*) The coach driver.

Desmond and David join them.

Desmond   You bought a lot, Mr Bourne. Ron wants to know if you want a hand unloading.

David   Yes, you should have seen the size of Mr Bourne's trolley at the hypermarket.

Mrs De S.   That does it. The Head will definitely be getting a phone call tomorrow.

Mr Bourne   Oh, dear.

The End

SPEAKING AND LISTENING ACTIVITIES

Help Notes can be found on pages 184–185.

FIRST DAY

INDIVIDUAL (Help Notes 1)

- **My First Day at School**. Prepare a short talk on your first day at school.
  Points to consider: first impressions, rules, playground, lunch, your feelings, excitement, nervousness, anxiety, fear, best bits, worst bits.

PAIRS (Help Notes 2)

- **Vegetarianism: For or Against**. Look at the conversation about food. One of you be in favour of vegetarianism and the other against.
  Points to consider: cruelty, expense, health, farmers' livelihoods, experiments on animals.
- **My Old School**. Interview each other about your old schools.

GROUP (Help Notes 2)

- **Racism in schools**. Schools have a statutory (legal) duty to provide a policy on how to combat racism. What do you think should be included in such a policy?

WRITING BASED ON ORAL ACTIVITIES

You can choose writing activities from this section that are based on oral work that you have done, or on the oral work of others that you have seen and made notes on. However, you can also choose activities for which you have had no oral preparation.

- Write a report for your old junior school about your experiences in your new school. (*Help Notes 3*)
- Write the arguments for and against Vegetarianism. (*Help Notes 4*)

SCHOOL PLAY

INDIVIDUAL (Help Notes 1)

- **Performance *or* Watching a Performance**. Prepare a short talk on performing in public, or watching a play. You could include: plays, musicals, concerts.
  Points to consider: Performance: things going wrong, excitement, fear, nervousness, exhilaration. Watching: summary, characters, your opinion.

PAIRS (Help Notes 2)

- **My Favourite Films and TV Programmes**. Interview each other about what films and TV programmes you like best. Try to talk more about your reasons than the storyline.

GROUP (Help Notes 2)

- **School Production**. Discuss all the aspects of putting on a school play, musical or concert.

WRITING BASED ON ORAL ACTIVITIES

You can choose writing activities from this section that are based on oral work that you have done, or on the oral work of others that you have seen and make notes on. However, you can also choose activities for which you have had no oral preparation.

- Write about your favourite film or TV programme. Don't just write the storyline. Say why you like it. (*Help Notes 4*)

GOOD FRIENDS

INDIVIDUAL (Help Notes 1)

- **My Leisure Activities**. Prepare a short talk about what you do in your spare time.
  Points to consider: how much time spent, in school or out of school, team or individual competitions, travel.

PAIRS (Help Notes 2)

- **The Right Punishment**. Each of you choose to be a character from the play. Have a conversation about the most appropriate punishment for Daniel, Gary and Karen.

- **Luxury Item**. Interview each other about what you would choose, and why, if you were allowed an expensive luxury item.

GROUP (Help Notes 2)

- **Stealing**. Two of you are accused of stealing from school. Your defence is. 'It's only borrowing. We were going to put it back.' Each of you accuses the other of being the ringleader. The rest are teachers who are trying to establish the truth.

- **True Friendship**. Discuss what true friendship means to you.

WRITING BASED ON ORAL ACTIVITIES

You can choose writing activities from this section that are based on oral work that you have done, or on the oral work of others that you have seen and made notes on. However, you can also choose activities for which you have had no oral preparation.

- Write a report for the school magazine describing your

hobby or leisure activity. (*Help Notes 3*)

- Writing as the two pupils who have been accused of stealing from school, produce a statement from each of them showing their versions of the story. These statements should show their different accounts of what happened. (*Help Notes 4*)

SCHOOL TRIP

INDIVIDUAL (Help Notes 1)

• **Holiday**. Prepare a short talk about a holiday that you have enjoyed.
  Points to consider: cost, places visited, food, language, high points, low points.

PAIRS (Help Notes 2)

• **My Dream Holiday**. Interview each other about where you would like to go for a dream holiday.

GROUP (Help Notes 2)

• **Field Trip**. Plan a school field trip and all its aspects. Think about:
    • where you are going
    • when you are going
    • why you are going (educational purposes)
    • how much it will cost
    • everyone's safety
    • what information you will need to give parents.

• **The Generation Gap**. Discuss the differences in outlook and attitude between the generations.

WRITING BASED ON ORAL ACTIVITIES

You can choose writing activities from this section that are based on oral work that you have done, or on the oral work of others that you have seen and made notes on. However, you can also choose activities for which you have had no oral preparation.

• Write a summary of the points made during the discussion on the Generation Gap. (*Help Notes 4*)

- Write a letter home to parents which gives all the details about a field trip that the school is planning. It may include dates, expense, location, purpose, educational content, travel and safety arrangements. (*Help Notes 5*)

HELP NOTES

1 INDIVIDUAL ORAL WORK

- Prepare well, and practise and time your talk.
- Don't write out the whole talk, or read it, or learn it off by heart.
- Use notes, and visual aids.
- Speak to the whole class, not just to the teacher, and try to stand still.
- Use a good vocabulary and avoid slang.
- Speak clearly and loudly for the whole of your allowed time.

2 PAIRS AND GROUP ORAL WORK

- Prepare well, have interesting content, and a good vocabulary.
- Divide the time equally between yourselves and listen carefully to one another.
- Encourage others to take part, especially those who are not saying much.
- Have a sensible seating arrangement and be aware of your audience.

3 REPORT WRITING

- Collect all the information you need and arrange it into categories.
- A report is not an essay. You can use sub-headings, graphs, lists and short points.
- A report uses formal language to state the facts. It may have a conclusion or recommendations at the end.

4 DISCURSIVE (ARGUMENTATIVE) WRITING

- Use different sources for your information, such as magazines, newspapers, videos, surveys.
- Some argumentative work will require you simply to state the facts For and Against. Or you may be asked to give your own opinion as well. Make sure you understand what you are being asked to do.
- Keep the facts separate from your opinions and include a brief introduction.
- In your conclusion briefly bring the main points together and, if required, give your own opinion.

5 LETTER WRITING

School Name
32 Banks Road
Anytown
Surrey AB1 2CD

Tel: 0181 123 4567

Date
Dear Parents,

We are writing to inform you ....

Yours sincerely,

(Signature)

DANIEL SMITH